Richard Ottinger (Ed.)

RELIGIOUS ELEMENTS IN THE RUSSIAN WAR OF AGGRESSION AGAINST UKRAINE

Propaganda, Religious Politics and Pastoral Care, 2014–2024

Bibliografische Information der Deutschen Nationalbibliothek
Die Deutsche Nationalbibliothek verzeichnet diese Publikation in der Deutschen Nationalbibliografie; detaillierte bibliografische Daten sind im Internet über http://dnb.d-nb.de abrufbar.

Bibliographic information published by the Deutsche Nationalbibliothek
The Deutsche Nationalbibliothek lists this publication in the Deutsche Nationalbibliografie; detailed bibliographic data are available on the Internet at http://dnb.d-nb.de.

Copy-editing: Academic Consulting Services Ltd., Oxford, UK

This volume has been published in cooperation with the Konrad-Adenauer-Stiftung.

ISBN (Print): 978-3-8382-1981-3
ISBN (E-Book [PDF]): 978-3-8382-7981-7
© *ibidem*-Verlag, Hannover • Stuttgart 2025

Alle Rechte vorbehalten

Leuschnerstraße 40
30457 Hannover
Germany / Deutschland
info@ibidem.eu

Das Werk einschließlich aller seiner Teile ist urheberrechtlich geschützt. Jede Verwertung außerhalb der engen Grenzen des Urheberrechtsgesetzes ist ohne Zustimmung des Verlages unzulässig und strafbar. Dies gilt insbesondere für Vervielfältigungen, Übersetzungen, Mikroverfilmungen und elektronische Speicherformen sowie die Einspeicherung und Verarbeitung in elektronischen Systemen.

All rights reserved. No part of this publication may be reproduced, stored in or introduced into a retrieval system, or transmitted, in any form, or by any means (electronic, mechanical, photocopying, recording or otherwise) without the prior written permission of the publisher. Any person who commits any unauthorized act in relation to this publication may be liable to criminal prosecution and civil claims for damages.

Printed in the EU

Soviet and Post-Soviet Politics and Society (SPPS) Vol. 286
ISSN 1614-3515

General Editor: Andreas Umland,
Stockholm Centre for Eastern European Studies, andreas.umland@ui.se

Commissioning Editor: Max Jakob Horstmann,
London, mjh@ibidem.eu

EDITORIAL COMMITTEE*

DOMESTIC & COMPARATIVE POLITICS
Prof. **Ellen Bos**, *Andrássy University of Budapest*
Dr. **Gergana Dimova**, *Florida State University*
Prof. **Heiko Pleines**, *University of Bremen*
Dr. **Sarah Whitmore**, *Oxford Brookes University*
Dr. **Harald Wydra**, *University of Cambridge*

SOCIETY, CLASS & ETHNICITY
Col. **David Glantz**, *"Journal of Slavic Military Studies"*
Dr. **Marlène Laruelle**, *George Washington University*
Dr. **Stephen Shulman**, *Southern Illinois University*
Prof. **Stefan Troebst**, *University of Leipzig*

POLITICAL ECONOMY & PUBLIC POLICY
Prof. **Andreas Goldthau**, *University of Erfurt*
Dr. **Robert Kravchuk**, *University of North Carolina*
Dr. **David Lane**, *University of Cambridge*
Dr. **Carol Leonard**, *University of Oxford*
Dr. **Maria Popova**, *McGill University, Montreal*

FOREIGN POLICY & INTERNATIONAL AFFAIRS
Dr. **Peter Duncan**, *University College London*
Prof. **Andreas Heinemann-Grüder**, *University of Bonn*
Prof. **Gerhard Mangott**, *University of Innsbruck*
Dr. **Diana Schmidt-Pfister**, *University of Konstanz*
Dr. **Lisbeth Tarlow**, *Harvard University, Cambridge*
Dr. **Christian Wipperfürth**, *N-Ost Network, Berlin*
Dr. **William Zimmerman**, *University of Michigan*

HISTORY, CULTURE & THOUGHT
Dr. **Catherine Andreyev**, *University of Oxford*
Prof. **Mark Bassin**, *Södertörn University*
Prof. **Karsten Brüggemann**, *Tallinn University*
Prof. **Alexander Etkind**, *Central European University*
Prof. **Gasan Gusejnov**, *Free University of Berlin*
Prof. **Leonid Luks**, *Catholic University of Eichstaett*
Dr. **Olga Malinova**, *Russian Academy of Sciences*
Dr. **Richard Mole**, *University College London*
Prof. **Andrei Rogatchevski**, *University of Tromsø*
Dr. **Mark Tauger**, *West Virginia University*

ADVISORY BOARD*

Prof. **Dominique Arel**, *University of Ottawa*
Prof. **Jörg Baberowski**, *Humboldt University of Berlin.*
Prof. **Margarita Balmaceda**, *Seton Hall University*
Dr. **John Barber**, *University of Cambridge*
Prof. **Timm Beichelt**, *European University Viadrina*
Dr. **Katrin Boeckh**, *University of Munich*
Prof. em. **Archie Brown**, *University of Oxford*
Dr. **Vyacheslav Bryukhovetsky**, *Kyiv-Mohyla Academy*
Prof. **Timothy Colton**, *Harvard University, Cambridge*
Prof. **Paul D'Anieri**, *University of California*
Dr. **Heike Dörrenbächer**, *Friedrich Naumann Foundation*
Dr. **John Dunlop**, *Hoover Institution, Stanford, California*
Dr. **Sabine Fischer**, *SWP, Berlin*
Dr. **Geir Flikke**, *NUPI, Oslo*
Prof. **David Galbreath**, *University of Aberdeen*
Prof. **Frank Golczewski**, *University of Hamburg*
Dr. **Nikolas Gvosdev**, *Naval War College, Newport, RI*
Prof. **Mark von Hagen**, *Arizona State University*
Prof. **Guido Hausmann**, *University of Regensburg*
Prof. **Dale Herspring**, *Kansas State University*
Dr. **Stefani Hoffman**, *Hebrew University of Jerusalem*
Prof. em. **Andrzej Korbonski**, *University of California*
Dr. **Iris Kempe**, *"Caucasus Analytical Digest"*
Prof. **Herbert Küpper**, *Institut für Ostrecht Regensburg*
Prof. **Rainer Lindner**, *University of Konstanz*

Dr. **Luke March**, *University of Edinburgh*
Prof. **Michael McFaul**, *Stanford University, Palo Alto*
Prof. **Birgit Menzel**, *University of Mainz-Germersheim*
Dr. **Alex Pravda**, *University of Oxford*
Dr. **Erik van Ree**, *University of Amsterdam*
Dr. **Joachim Rogall**, *Robert Bosch Foundation Stuttgart*
Prof. **Peter Rutland**, *Wesleyan University, Middletown*
Prof. **Gwendolyn Sasse**, *University of Oxford*
Prof. **Jutta Scherrer**, *EHESS, Paris*
Prof. **Robert Service**, *University of Oxford*
Mr. **James Sherr**, *RIIA Chatham House London*
Dr. **Oxana Shevel**, *Tufts University, Medford*
Prof. **Eberhard Schneider**, *University of Siegen*
Prof. **Olexander Shnyrkov**, *Shevchenko University, Kyiv*
Prof. **Hans-Henning Schröder**, *SWP, Berlin*
Prof. **Yuri Shapoval**, *Ukrainian Academy of Sciences*
Dr. **Lisa Sundstrom**, *University of British Columbia*
Dr. **Philip Walters**, *"Religion, State and Society", Oxford*
Prof. **Zenon Wasyliw**, *Ithaca College, New York State*
Dr. **Lucan Way**, *University of Toronto*
Dr. **Markus Wehner**, *"Frankfurter Allgemeine Zeitung"*
Dr. **Andrew Wilson**, *University College London*
Prof. **Jan Zielonka**, *University of Oxford*
Prof. **Andrei Zorin**, *University of Oxford*

---

* While the Editorial Committee and Advisory Board support the General Editor in the choice and improvement of manuscripts for publication, responsibility for remaining errors and misinterpretations in the series' volumes lies with the books' authors.

Soviet and Post-Soviet Politics and Society (SPPS)
ISSN 1614-3515

Founded in 2004 and refereed since 2007, SPPS makes available affordable English-, German-, and Russian-language studies on the history of the countries of the former Soviet bloc from the late Tsarist period to today. It publishes between 5 and 20 volumes per year and focuses on issues in transitions to and from democracy such as economic crisis, identity formation, civil society development, and constitutional reform in CEE and the NIS. SPPS also aims to highlight so far understudied themes in East European studies such as right-wing radicalism, religious life, higher education, or human rights protection. The authors and titles of all previously published volumes are listed at the end of this book. For a full description of the series and reviews of its books, see www.ibidem-verlag.de/red/spps.

Editorial correspondence & manuscripts should be sent to: Dr. Andreas Umland, Department of Political Science, Kyiv-Mohyla Academy, vul. Voloska 8/5, UA-04070 Kyiv, UKRAINE; andreas.umland@cantab.net

Business correspondence & review copy requests should be sent to: *ibidem* Press, Leuschnerstr. 40, 30457 Hannover, Germany; tel.: +49 511 2622200; fax: +49 511 2622201; spps@ibidem.eu.

Authors, reviewers, referees, and editors for (as well as all other persons sympathetic to) SPPS are invited to join its networks at www.facebook.com/group.php?gid=52638198614
www.linkedin.com/groups?about=&gid=103012
www.xing.com/net/spps-ibidem-verlag/

Recent Volumes

277 Gian Marco Moisé
The House Always Wins
The Corrupt Strategies that Shaped Kazakh Oil Politics and Business in the Nazarbayev Era
With a foreword by Alena Ledeneva
ISBN 978-3-8382-1917-2

278 Mikhail Minakov
The Post-Soviet Human
Philosophical Reflections on Social History after the End of Communism
ISBN 978-3-8382-1943-1

279 Natalia Kudriavtseva, Debra A. Friedman (eds.)
Language and Power in Ukraine and Kazakhstan
Essays on Education, Ideology, Literature, Practice, and the Media
With a foreword by Laada Bilaniuk
ISBN 978-3-8382-1949-3

280 Georges Mink, Iwona Reichardt (eds.)
The End of the Soviet World?
Essays on Post-Communist Political and Social Change
With an afterword by Richardt Butterwick
ISBN 978-3-8382-1961-5

281 Kateryna Zarembo, Michèle Knodt, Maksym Yakovlyev (eds.)
Teaching IR in Wartime
Experiences of University Lecturers during Russia's Full-Scale Invasion of Ukraine
ISBN 978-3-8382-1954-7

282 Oleksiy V. Kresin
The United Nations General Assembly Resolutions
Their Nature and Significance in the Context of the Russian War Against Ukraine
Edited by William E. Butler
ISBN 978-3-8382-1967-7

283 Jakob Hauter
Russlands unbemerkte Invasion
Die Ursachen des Kriegsausbruchs im ukrainischen Donbas im Jahr 2014
Mit einem Vorwort von Hiroaki Kuromiya
ISBN 978-3-8382-2003-1

284 „Alles kann sich ändern"
Letzte Worte politisch Angeklagter vor Gericht in Russland
Herausgegeben von Memorial Deutschland e.V.
ISBN 978-3-8382-1994-3

285 Nadiya Kiss, Monika Wingender (Eds.)
Contested Language Diversity in Contemporary Ukraine
National Minorities, Language Biographies, and Linguistic Landscape
ISBN 978-3-8382-1966-0

Contents

Introduction: The Russian War of Aggression Against Ukraine: Not a War of Religion, but a Religious War
Richard Ottinger 7

The Church Dispute in Ukraine and the State's Religious Policy: Are Concerns Over Religious Freedom Justified?
Johannes Oeldemann 13

War Propaganda and '*Russki Mir*': The Russian Orthodox Church as an Emissary for Imperial Ambitions?
Andreas Heinemann-Grüder 23

The Russian Invasion and World Orthodoxy: A Geopolitical Schism?
Thomas Bremer 31

Jewish Life in Russia and Ukraine: A Paradigm Shift Since the Invasion?
Pinchas Goldschmidt 39

Papal Diplomacy for Ukraine: Naïve Pacifism or Strategic Neutrality?
Ludwig Ring-Eifel 45

Ukrainian Churches and Religious Communities in the Invasion: Overlooked Contributions?
Vladyslav Zaiets 55

Ukrainian Free Churches after the Invasion: The Power of National Reinvention?
Joshua T. Searle and Oleksandr Geychenko 65

Islam and Muslims in the Russian War of Aggression: Jihad Against Ukraine?
Andreas Jacobs 77

Military Chaplaincy on the Front Line: Theological Practice in the Horror of War?
Regina Elsner 87

'*Just War*' and '*Emergency Aid*': Obsolete or Key Categories for the War in Ukraine?
Franz-Josef Bormann 97

On the Contributors 107

Introduction
The Russian War of Aggression Against Ukraine: Not a War of Religion, but a Religious War

Richard Ottinger

The war that Russia has been waging against Ukraine since 2014 and dramatically escalated with the invasion in 2022 is not a religious war. Nevertheless, religious elements play a remarkable but often overlooked role in the genesis and course of the war. Isolated studies of religious facets of the war have already been conducted, but a systematic overview of the various religious aspects of the Russian war of aggression against Ukraine has yet to be compiled. This anthology aims to close this research gap and offers an interdisciplinary overview.

In the first article, theologian Johannes Oeldemann focuses on Ukraine and highlights that the conflict with Russia had already begun on a religious-political level long before the 2022 invasion. With the founding of the Orthodox Church of Ukraine (OCU) against the Ukrainian Orthodox Church (UOC), which belongs to the Russian Orthodox Church (ROC), a church dispute broke out in Ukraine in 2018 that remains unresolved to this day. Despite distancing itself from Russia and condemning the invasion, the UOC has not been able to convince its critics of the opposite, who continue to accuse it of loyalty to Russia. The result of this persistent mistrust is evident in a draft bill that contains a ban on religious organisations whose centre is located in an 'aggressor state'. This was adopted at second reading on 20 August 2024. Oeldemann denies the accusation frequently voiced by international observers of a comprehensive restriction of the human right to freedom of religion and belief in Ukraine, but points out the negative consequences of state interference in church matters and the danger to social cohesion.

Political scientist Andreas Heinemann-Grüder examines the power of the 'Russki-Mir ideology', which is disseminated via networks controlled by the Kremlin. The aim of this—deliberately vague—religiously induced propaganda is to bind people living outside Russia to the Russian state and its ideology. The various narratives of the 'Russian world' are held together by anti-Western justifications for the invasion and ultimately the aim of weakening the West by actively dividing their societies. The analysis shows the connections between the ROC and the Kremlin as well as their function in the context of spreading Russian propaganda.

The third article focuses on the consequences of the Ukrainian church dispute and the Russian war of aggression for world Orthodoxy. From an ecumenical perspective, Eastern Church expert Thomas Bremer shows that the impact of the conflict between churches has led to a split in the Orthodox Christian churches as a whole, far beyond the country's borders. The fault lines in the assessment of the church dispute and the invasion largely align with the old patriarchates (Alexandria, Antioch, Jerusalem) taking different positions. With regard to the communion of the world Orthodoxy, the unilateral withdrawal of the ROC is striking. Almost all other Orthodox churches remain in communion with each other despite their sometimes decidedly different stances on the war. Bremer's contextualisation makes it clear that Russia's invasion is part of a multi-dimensional aggression that began long before 2014 or 2022.

The Chief Rabbi of Moscow in exile, Pinchas Goldschmidt, describes the start of the Russian invasion of Ukraine in 2022 as the end of the renaissance of Russian Jewry. This paradigm shift for Jewish life in Russia is characterised by explosive anti-Semitism and, as a result, a mass exodus of more than a third of all Jewish Russians. He describes in detail the shift in power between the Jewish actors in Russia after the start of the invasion and the growing tensions between Russia and Israel. These developments sharply contrast with a Ukraine led by a Jewish president and in which people of the Jewish faith are naturally protected by the human right to freedom of religion and belief.

The journalist Ludwig Ring-Eifel provides a snapshot analysis of the Vatican's diplomacy in the context of the war. He notes that, unlike his predecessors during the Cold War, the Pope did not act as an ally of the West. He attributes this to the fact that Francis does not appear to see Russia as an ideological opponent. Whereas the Soviet Union was primarily atheist, Russia today, with the help of the ROC, is presenting itself aggressively as Christian. Instead of clearly naming the aggressor, Francis views the war more from the perspective of a 'prophet of world peace' and a 'world war warner'. Ring-Eifel examines the Pope's use or non-use of the Vatican infrastructure and describes the unusual situation in which the Pope's statements have to be regularly re-explained, from the press spokesman to the nuncio in Kiev. According to Ring-Eifel, it seems unlikely that the Pope will change his position in the near future.

In the following article, legal scholar Vladyslav Zaiets offers a comprehensive overview regarding the activities of often overlooked religious communities in Ukraine. He is particularly interested in the endeavours of the Ukrainian Greek Catholic, Roman Catholic and Protestant churches as well as the Muslim, Jewish and Buddhist communities in the country. It makes it clear that the smaller religious communities in Ukraine also make an important contribution to pastoral care and stand up for social cohesion. They enjoy high levels of public trust and are well connected internationally. The article also visualises the often overlooked religious heterogeneity of Ukraine and interprets the activities of smaller religious communities in the country as an integral part of Ukraine's support and reconstruction efforts. The Russian war of aggression also becomes recognisable here as a systemic struggle of religious freedom against religious unfreedom.

Theologians Joshua T. Searle and Oleksandr Geychenko also support this interpretation of a systemic conflict in their article on the free churches in Ukraine and Russia. In Ukraine, Free Church congregations can live out their claim to freedom, whereas in Russia they represent an oppressed minority which, unlike the ROC, is not identified with the Russian national image. The authors emphasise the role of the Ukrainian free churches in the creation of

Ukraine's new national and European identity. They cite the genuinely Free Church rejection of external control as the reason for the new resonance with the public and the support of the Ukrainian population, which took on a new meaning in the context of the Russian attack. Searle and Geychenko argue that the war between Russia and Ukraine also represents a conflict between a self-determined 'public Christianity' and an instrumentalised 'state-sponsored Christianity'.

The article by political scientist and Islamic scholar Andreas Jacobs also focuses on state-sponsored religion. He explains the foreign and domestic policy impact of Russian Islam policy and the contribution of Islam in the context of the invasion. Chechen President Ramzan Kadyrov stands at the core of Russia's Islam policy. His specific interpretation of Islam ('Kadyrovism') helps the Putin regime to control domestic political opponents and, analogous to the 'Russki Mir' concept, to proclaim Islam as constitutive for Russia and to provide fighters for the front. The Islamist and nationalist propaganda unites the anti-Western narrative. At the same time, this strategy also carries risks for Russia, as this specifically Russian Islam provokes jihadist terrorists and fuels internal Muslim rivalries.

Theologian Regina Elsner compares Ukrainian and Russian military chaplaincy on the front line. Interreligiousness and religious freedom are crucial for military chaplaincy in Ukraine. In addition, the role of chaplains and soldiers is strictly delineated in Ukraine, as chaplains are not allowed to serve in the armed forces and the promotion of patriotism is not part of their remit. In contrast, chaplaincy in Russia is characterised by a theology of war in which religious freedom plays no role, the ROC is prioritised and the focus is on the service to the fatherland combined with constant self-sacrifice. Elsner works out the structural differences between the opponents' views of the world and image of man. Her analysis highlights the front between Russian Orthodox imperialist propaganda and multi-religious support for the soldiers.

This anthology concludes with the ethicist Franz-Josef Bormann's examination of the connection between the traditional doctrine of 'just war' and the Russian invasion. Bormann clarifies how under-complex the equation of Christianity with pacifism is and points out the frequently repeated mistake of proclaiming an alleged contradiction between 'ius ad bellum' and peace ethics. According to Bormann, the model of just peace is neither a contradiction nor an alternative to the doctrine of just war. On the contrary, the former complements the latter with elements of a policy that prevents violence. The frequent accusation of Western double standards in addressing conflicts that take place in the immediate vicinity can be classified with Bormann's reference to the concept of the 'ordo caritatis'. By distinguishing between self-defence and emergency aid presented here, he provides ethical tools for an in-depth examination of the Russian invasion and the support of the attacked.

The variety of contributions in this anthology illustrates how religion functions in the context of war as a propaganda tool, a source of motivation and a source of hope. The religious elements in the Russian war of aggression against Ukraine are thus exemplary of the different roles played by religion worldwide. However, the anthology is also indicative of a continuously secularising West, which primarily emphasises the negative impact of religion and often overlooks or at least underestimates the potential of religion to pacify societies and international relations. At a time when signs of a possible shift in US policy towards Ukraine are emerging Ukraine and when Volodymyr Zelensky is talking publicly for the first time about the possibility of ceding territory, it seems necessary to reflect again on the creative potential of religion for Ukraine's future. The high reputation, the proximity to the people in the country and the ability to address existential issues make churches and religious communities in Ukraine predestined partners for the management of a ceasefire and possibly a post-military conflict. An institutional starting point could be the 'All-Ukrainian Council of Churches and

Religious Organizations' established in 1996, under whose umbrella almost all religious communities are gathered. From here, multi-religious post-war pastoral care could be coordinated and new impulses for transitional reconstruction could be developed. In this context, it might also be helpful to re-evaluate the Ukrainian church dispute. Given the extensive suffering inflicted on the Ukrainian people by the Russian invaders, which will presumably continue to have an impact for generations, it would be irresponsible not to utilise all instruments, actors and possibilities to resolve the conflict sustainably: Including, of course, religion.

Berlin, December 9, 2024

The Church Dispute in Ukraine and the State's Religious Policy
Are Concerns Over Religious Freedom Justified?

Johannes Oeldemann

Ukraine was and is—as the Slavic root of the country's name implies—a "borderland": politically between East and West, ecclesiastically between Constantinople, Moscow and Rome. This is reflected on the one hand in the changing political affiliation of the territory of today's Ukraine, and on the other in the confessional and religious diversity that has characterized the country for centuries.[1] Around two thirds of the population belong to the Orthodox Church, but Ukraine is not an "Orthodox" country in which Orthodoxy alone dominates the religious landscape. This can be seen in the composition of the "Ukrainian Council of Churches and Religious Organizations"[2], which includes not only many Christian churches, but also representatives of Judaism and Islam.

Ukrainian Orthodoxy between Moscow and Constantinople

Immediately after Ukraine's declaration of independence and the dissolution of the Soviet Union, a "break from Moscow" movement

---

[1] See Boeckh, Katrin, and Oleh Turij, eds. Religiöse Pluralität als Faktor des Politischen in der Ukraine. Regensburg, 2015; Heyer, Friedrich. Kirchengeschichte der Ukraine im 20. Jahrhundert. Göttingen, 2003; Bremer, Thomas. "Religion in Ukraine: Historical Background and Present Situation." In Churches in the Ukrainian Crisis, edited by Andrii Krawchuk and Thomas Bremer, New York, 2016, 3-20.

[2] See UCCRO. "Information about UCCRO" https://vrciro.org.ua/en/council/info. On the significance of this advice see Vasyn, Maksym. "Ukrainian Council of Churches and Religious Organizations as a Voice for Justice and Humanity during the Russian Invasion." Review of Ecumenical Studies 15 (2023): 429-458.

within the Ukrainian Orthodox Church emerged, which led to several competing Orthodox church structures.³ The Ukrainian Autocephalous Orthodox Church (UAOC) and the "Kyiv Patriarchate" (KP) led by the self-appointed "Patriarch" Filaret (Denysenko) were regarded as schismatic churches within the Orthodox Church as a whole. Only the "Ukrainian Orthodox Church" (UOC), which belonged to the Moscow Patriarchate and was granted extensive autonomy from Moscow in 1992, was accepted within the Orthodox Church as a "canonical" (legitimate) church. Little changed in this respect for around 25 years. Individual initiatives for talks between representatives of the various Orthodox jurisdictions failed and Moscow showed little interest in accommodating the "schismatics" in any way.

This situation changed in 2018, partly due to the political ambitions of then Ukrainian President Petro Poroshenko, who hoped that his advocacy of an autocephalous church independent of Moscow would provide a tailwind for his upcoming re-election in spring 2019. In April 2018, he traveled to Istanbul to lobby the Ecumenical Patriarchate—supported by a corresponding parliamentary resolution—for the autocephaly of the Orthodox Church in Ukraine. The fact that Poroshenko, unlike previous Ukrainian presidents, found open ears in Constantinople has to do with certain ecclesiastical political motives, which were the second decisive factor. The Patriarchate of Constantinople wanted to emphasize its leading role within the Orthodox church worldwide and demonstrate this by overcoming the long-standing intra-Ukrainian schism.⁴ An important psychological factor in this context was the fact that the Moscow Patriarchate had canceled its participation in the "Holy and Great Synod" of the Orthodox Church in Crete (June 2016) two years earlier, which was a matter close to the heart of

---

3   See Denysenko, Nicholas. The Orthodox Church in Ukraine: A Century of Separation. DeKalb, IL, 2018.
4   Regarding the position of the Patriarchate of Constantinople in the Ukrainian church dispute see Sotiropoulos, Evagelos, ed. "The Ecumenical Patriarchate and Ukraine Autocephaly: Historical, Canonical, and Pastoral Perspectives" May 2019. https://archons.org/wp-content/uploads/2024/01/eBook-Ukraine-FINAL.pdf.

Ecumenical Patriarch Bartholomew. After this disappointment, he was no longer willing to show consideration for Moscow and sought a solution to the Ukrainian church issue without consulting the Moscow Patriarch.

Constantinople's original intention was to reunite the three competing Orthodox church structures in Ukraine into one church and then grant it autocephaly (ecclesiastical independence).[5] This initiative was based on the hope that the prospect of autocephaly would be so attractive to all those involved that they would put aside their internal disputes in order to achieve this goal. However, this hope was not fulfilled. The "Unification Council" convened on December 15, 2018, in the historic St. Sophia Cathedral in Kyiv was attended by all the bishops of the UAOC and the KP, but only two bishops of the UOC. All other UOC bishops stayed away from the council. Nevertheless, Patriarch Bartholomew decided to present the "Tomos" (certificate) of autocephaly to the head of the newly founded "Orthodox Church of Ukraine", Metropolitan Epiphanij (Dumenko), on January 6, 2019.[6]

Since then, there have been two competing Orthodox church structures in Ukraine: the "Orthodox Church of Ukraine" (OCU) under the leadership of Metropolitan Epifanij, which is in communion with the Patriarchate of Constantinople, and the "Ukrainian Orthodox Church" (UOC) under the leadership of Metropolitan Onufrij (Berezovskij), which was subject to the Patriarchate of Moscow until May 2022.[7]

The other Orthodox churches largely observed the intensifying dispute between Constantinople and Moscow with restraint

---

5   See Elsner, Regina. "Autokephalie der ukrainischen Orthodoxie: Die Politisierung der Kirchen im postsowjetischen Raum." In Politische Macht und orthodoxer Glaube: Beziehungen zwischen Politik und Religion in Osteuropa, edited by Marco Besl and Simone Oelke, Regensburg, 2023, 53–68.
6   On these events and the motives of those involved, see Oeldemann, Johannes. "Orthodoxe Kirchen in der Ukraine: Zum Spannungsfeld zwischen Konstantinopel und Moskau." Stimmen der Zeit 237, no. 4 (2019): 279–294.
7   For an assessment of this situation, see Bremer, Thomas, and Sophia Senyk. "The Current Ecclesial Situation in Ukraine: Critical Remarks." St. Vladimir's Theological Quarterly 63 (2019): 27–58.

and tried to avoid taking a clear position.[8] The newly founded OCU has so far only been officially recognized by four Orthodox churches (Constantinople, Alexandria, Cyprus, Greece), which are led by bishops from the Greek cultural area. Bishops from these churches who concelebrated with OCU bishops were sanctioned by the Moscow Patriarchate. This conflict is most evident on the African continent, where the Moscow Patriarchate has begun to establish parallel structures to the Patriarchate of Alexandria, whose "canonical territory"[9] Africa was previously considered to be unchallenged.

The church dispute in Ukraine

In Ukraine itself, in the first weeks after the conferral of autocephaly on the OCU, some Orthodox parishes from the UOC was the OCU, which gained obviously supported by Ukrainian-nationalist forces. It was reported several times that large groups of people who had not previously participated in the religious life of the congregation came unexpectedly and apparently in an organized manner to congregational meetings at which a decision was to be made about the affiliation of the congregation. They ensured that the majority of the congregation voted in favor of the change to the OCU. As a result, the keys to the church were handed over to a representative of this church, while the UOC priest had to celebrate the liturgy from then on with the regular worshippers in the rectory or other locations such as a garage. Although a three-digit number of parishes changed jurisdiction in this way, it was not a mass movement from the "old" to the "new" Orthodox Church in Ukraine, given that there were more than 12,000 UOC parishes throughout Ukraine. When President Volodymyr Zelensky took office, political support for this

---

8   On the effects of the Ukrainian church dispute on Orthodoxy as a whole, see Bremer, Thomas et al., eds. Orthodoxy in Two Manifestations? The Conflict in Ukraine as Expression of a Fault Line in World Orthodoxy. Berlin, 2022.

9   On the concept of "canonical territory", see Oeldemann, Johannes. "Canonical Territory: A New Paradigm of Orthodox Ecclesiology with Ancient Roots." In Autocephaly: Coming of Age in Communion. Historical, Canonical, Liturgical, and Theological Studies, edited by Edward G. Farrugia and Zeljko Paša, Rome, 2023, 1159–1190.

change of parishes initially ended, meaning that the number of transfer of parishes fell significantly in the second half of 2019.[10] At the level of the priesthood, there were various attempts to initiate a dialog between the two Orthodox churches in Ukraine, but these failed.[11]

The large-scale invasion of Ukraine by Russian troops since February 24, 2022 also led to a new dynamic in the Ukrainian church dispute—with opposing tendencies in the church policy orientation of the Orthodox bishops and the religious policy activities of the political rulers. The UOC, which was originally associated with Moscow, is one of the churches most affected by the invasion because it is more widespread in eastern Ukraine than in the west. In the first year of the Russian invasion alone, more than 200 UOC church buildings were destroyed,[12] although one of Moscow's ostensible reasons for the invasion was to protect "Russian" believers in Ukraine. The head of the UOC, Metropolitan Onufrij, expressed his criticism of Moscow's attack on February 24, 2022, the first day of the invasion, and called for the defense of Ukraine. Three months after the war of aggression began, on May 27, 2022, a council of the UOC convened at short notice declared the "complete independence" of the Ukrainian Orthodox Church from Moscow and removed all references to the Moscow Patriarchate from the church's statutes.[13]

---

10 On the developments from 2019 to 2022, see the Forum RGOW dossier on Ukrainian Orthodoxy "Von der Gründung der OKU bis zum Angriffskrieg." Dossier des Forums RGOW zur ukrainischen Orthodoxie (2019–2022). https://rgow.eu/zeitschrift/themendossiers/ukrainische-orthodoxie-von-der-gruendung-der-oku-bis-zum-angriffskrieg.

11 See Dudchenko, Andriy. "An Unofficial UOC-OCU Dialogue as a Grassroots Initiative for Reconciliation of the Orthodoxy in Ukraine." Review of Ecumenical Studies 15 (2023): 563–571.

12 See the report by Ziuzina, Anna Mariya Basauri, et al. Religion on Fire. https://www.mar.in.ua/wp-content/uploads/2023/04/Religion-on-Fire-report-2023-ENG.pdf. For the significance of this report, see Ziuzina, Anna Mariya Basauri, et al. "The Impact of War on Christian Communities in Ukraine (Based on Materials from the Religion on Fire Project)." Review of Ecumenical Studies 15 (2023): 405–428.

13 See "Die Kirchen und der Krieg in der Ukraine (Chronik)." Orthodoxes Forum 36 (2022): 143–158.

The canonical status of the UOC has been unclear ever since: on the one hand, the UOC avoids declaring itself "autocephalous" because this would probably not be recognized by either Moscow or Constantinople. On the other hand, the hierarchy of the church behaves in many respects as an autocephalous church would: the head of the church is mentioned in all services in the high prayer, Metropolitan Onufrij has consecrated the myron (anointing oil) himself and the UOC is founding its own congregations abroad, primarily to provide pastoral care for the numerous refugees from Ukraine.

State religious policy and the question of religious freedom

Despite this clear distancing from the Moscow Patriarchate and Russian religious policy, the UOC is accused by the state of continuing to have links with Moscow and undermining the "spiritual sovereignty" of Ukraine.[14] Some representatives of the UOC have been accused of collaborating with Moscow in trials and some have been sentenced to prison.[15] President Zelensky has abandoned his initial neutrality on religious issues and is also critical of the UOC. This has encouraged local politicians to take tougher action against the UOC and to promote the transfer of congregations and church buildings from the UOC to the OCU. A particularly symbolic place in this context is the Kyiv Cave Monastery, which is considered the spiritual center of Ukrainian Orthodoxy. The buildings of the cave monastery, which bears the honorary title of a "Lavra" (grand monastery), have belonged to the state since the Soviet era, but had been left to the UOC for use since Ukraine's independence. The state museum administration terminated the contract for the use of the lavra at the beginning of March 2023 and initially made the large cathedral in the "upper lavra" available to the OCU for religious services.

---

14 See Koshkina, Sonya. "Ukrainian Orthodoxy after the Start of Russia's Great War against Ukraine." Review of Ecumenical Studies 15 (2023): 550–562.
15 See "UOK-Bischof zu Haftstrafe verurteilt." August 24, 2023. https://noek.inf o/nachrichten/osteuropa/ukraine/3018-ukraine-uok-bischof-zu-haftstrafe-ve rurteilt.

There were more heated disputes over the buildings in the "lower Lavra", which not only houses the monks of the cave monastery, but also the church administration and theological schools (seminary and academy) of the UOC. Angry believers prevented the handover of the buildings as demanded by the state.[16] The Theological Academy has since moved to another monastery, while the monks continue to live in the cave monastery. Despite massive political pressure, only one of the monks converted to the OCU, who was then immediately appointed archimandrite (head of the monastery) by the church leadership.

While the highly symbolic dispute over the cave monastery quickly attracted attention in the international media, a legislative project being discussed by the Ukrainian parliament, which poses a much greater long-term threat to the UOC, was largely only noticed in specialist circles. The draft law, which bore the number 8371 in the parliamentary consultation process, provides for a ban on religious organizations whose center is located in an "aggressor state". It was discussed at first reading by the Rada, the Ukrainian parliament, in October 2023. The UOC, which the law aims to ban, sought legal advice from the international law firm Amsterdam & Partners. As a result, the revision of the law was repeatedly delayed and its second reading in parliament was postponed several times. Over the course of time, the draft bill became an extensive volume, which—in a comparative presentation of the various versions—comprises 916 pages.[17] Representatives of the UOC warned that

---

16 For classification see Denysenko, Nicholas. "Drama at the Lavra: What's at Stake?" April 10, 2023. https://publicorthodoxy.org/2023/04/10/drama-at-the-lavra/.
17 See the analyses by Peter Anderson: "Peter Anderson berichtet aus der orthodoxen Welt. 21 January 2024: New legal analysis of Ukrainian Draft Law 8371" https://www.unifr.ch/orthodoxia/de/dokumentation/anderson/; "Peter Anderson berichtet aus der orthodoxen Welt. 6 March 2024: Rada committee approves 'stronger' version of 8371 & other news" https://www.unifr.ch/orthodoxia/de/dokumentation/anderson/; "Peter Anderson berichtet aus der orthodoxen Welt. 13 May 2024: English translation of full text of latest version of 8371 & commentary" https://www.unifr.ch/orthodoxia/de/dokumentation/anderson/; "Peter Anderson berichtet aus der orthodoxen Welt. 22 July 2024: Concealment continues—Draft Law 8371" https://www.unifr.ch/orthodoxia/de/dokumentation/anderson/.

passing the law would massively restrict religious freedom in Ukraine. Western observers partly agreed with this argument, but at the same time pointed out that religious freedom in the Russian-occupied areas of Ukraine was much more at risk than in Ukraine as a whole.[18] There, however, it is not the UOC but the OCU that is counted among the churches suppressed by the state (in this case: the Russian side).

Despite international criticism, the Ukrainian parliament adopted the draft law at second reading on August 20, 2024. Just four days later, on Ukraine's Independence Day (August 24), it was signed by President Zelensky and came into force 30 days later. The date of signing underlines the highly symbolic significance of this law as a sign of independence from Moscow, including in the religious sphere. The law does not constitute a direct "ban" on the UOC, as this would be difficult to implement in legal terms, as the UOC cannot be banned as a church as a whole but would have to be banned for each individual parish and each diocese in a separate legal procedure. The adopted law, which now bears the number 3894 and is entitled "On the protection of the constitutional order in the area of the activities of religious organizations",[19] provides for a transitional period of nine months, which should enable the parishes and dioceses of the UOC to break away from the Moscow Patriarchate during this time. If they do not want to enter an ecclesiastical no-man's land (in theological terminology: a schism), they are practically forced to join the OCU. The law may not endanger religious freedom in Ukraine as a whole, but it proves that the state's religious policy is massively interfering in church issues and attempting to strengthen the OCU and weaken the UOC. In doing so, the state is deepening the division between the two Orthodox

---

18 See for example the statement of the Church of England: Church of England, General Synod. The War in Ukraine and the Challenge to International Order. February 2024, No. 15–21. https://www.churchofengland.org/sites/default/files/2024-02/gs-2348-war-in-ukraine-final-final.pdf.

19 See the official version of the legal text: "Закон України. Про захист конституційного ладу у сфері діяльності релігійних організацій". August 20, 2024. https://zakon.rada.gov.ua/laws/show/3894-20#Text.

churches in Ukraine and jeopardizing social cohesion, which is more important than ever in the face of Russian aggression.

Conclusion

The Ukrainian church dispute is based on a conglomerate of church political motives and state interests, which is likely to be counterproductive for all parties involved in the long term. The triggering factor was the Moscow Patriarchate's claim, linked to the idea of the "Russian world", that Ukraine belongs to its "canonical territory". Moscow's stance was ultimately based on the idea of the "symphony" of state and church, which was adopted from the Byzantine Empire. This model has been discredited by the church leadership in Moscow's support for the Russian war of aggression.[20] However, the underlying idea of close cooperation between state and church is still alive in the Patriarchate of Constantinople, as the process of granting autocephaly to the "Orthodox Church of Ukraine" shows. Finally, with its clear preference for the OCU and its activities directed against the UOC, the Ukrainian state is also following the traditional pattern of relations between state and church in the Orthodox world.

The dispute over the Orthodox Church in Ukraine will therefore not come to an end in the near future. Because in the situation of war, both Russia and Ukraine are trying to appropriate the religious forces in society in their own interests. Religion in general and the Orthodox Church in particular are being instrumentalized in this way and delegitimized in the eyes of many believers. The long-term impact this will have on the religious landscape in Ukraine is not yet foreseeable. However, it is to be feared that the formative and spiritual power of the churches will be damaged by the politicization of religion. A redefinition of the relationship between state and church (not only) in Ukraine would be forward-looking, so that

---

20 See Oeldemann, Johannes. "Towards an End of the 'Byzantine' Model? Church and State in the Orthodox World in the Light of the War in Ukraine." One in Christ 56 (2022): 44–65.

the Orthodox Church can find its socially recognized role in a religiously and ideologically pluralistic state, as Ukraine has historically been.

War Propaganda and *'Russki Mir'*
The Russian Orthodox Church as an Emissary for Imperial Ambitions?

Andreas Heinemann-Grüder

The term "Russian World" refers to an obscure but powerful ideology combining "soft power" or "sharp power" tactics with "hard power" strategies that is spread via networks controlled by the Kremlin to bind people living outside Russia to the Russian state and its ideological framework. The "Russian world" is striving for a "pan-Russian" unification of Russia, Belarus, and Ukraine into one state and an expansion of Russian influence in countries with a significant Russian-speaking population, including the Baltic states and Germany.[1] It promotes an independent civilization based on common origins, religion, and historical heritage. Revived under the Putin regime this ideology has enriched its propaganda with a mixture of anti-Western narratives, orthodox dogma, victim narratives, conspiracy theories and the myth of the strong state.

The concept of the "Russian world" comprises three dimensions: (1) strategic narratives to gain an audience, especially in Europe, and justifications for the war against Ukraine; (2) resentment, emotional appeals and offers of identification and; (3) the institutions, resources, and media to spread the ideology. The Russian Federation created a network of organizations that influence the Russian-speaking population in EU countries to exert "sharp

---

1   See Tishkov, Valerij A. Russkii mir. Rossiiskii narod: Istorija i smysl natsionalnogo samosoznaniya. Moskau, 2013.; Suslov, Mikhail. "'Russian World' Concept: Post-Soviet Geopolitical Ideology and the Logic of 'Spheres of Influence.'" Geopolitics 23, no. 2 (2018): 330–53; Laruelle, Marlene. The "Russian World": Russia's Soft Power and Geopolitical Imagination. Washington, DC: Center on Global Interests, 2015; Batanova, Ol'ga N. Russkii mir i problemy ego formirovaniya v sovremennykh usloviyakh. Moskau, 2009; Eltchaninoff, Michel. In Putins Kopf. Logik und Willkür eines Autokraten. Bonn, 2022; Bluhm, Katharina. Russland und der Westen. Berlin, 2023.

power", including strategic narratives, the exploitation of asymmetric information access (both in free and autocratic states), the use of symbolic violence (violent symbolism and threats of violence), the division of the public in the target country, the manipulation and masquerade of information, and manipulative information management and subversive activities.[2]

In the 1990s, so-called "methodologists" introduced the term "Russian world", including spin doctors and politicians such as the journalist Gleb Pavlovsky, the philosopher Georgy Shchedrovitsky and senior state officials such as Yuri Krupnov and Sergei Kirienko (head of the Russian presidential administration and now curator of the Russian-occupied territories of Ukraine). The "methodologists" understood the "Russian world" as a network of Russian-affiliated communities abroad.

Starting with Vladimir Putin's first presidency (in 2000), Russian authorities began to apply the term to the so-called "compatriots" or Russian-speaking minorities living outside Russia after the collapse of the USSR.[3] At the heart of the "Russian World" is the idea of protecting the rights of so-called "compatriots", i.e. members of the Russian diaspora or Russian-speaking minorities who feel a connection to the Russian language and culture. The "Russian world" became the ideological basis for diaspora policy. In 2006, Putin declared: *"The Russian World can and must unite all those who care about the Russian word and Russian culture, no matter where they live, in Russia or abroad."*[4]

To this day, the Orthodox churches, and the Russian surnames of indigenous inhabitants even in Alaska bear witness to this legacy. Since the "Russian world" does not stop at the borders of the Russian Federation, Russian political technologists use the Russian-speaking population abroad as a tool to influence politics.

---

2 See Dreyer, June T. "Roundtable on Sharp Power, Soft Power, and the Challenge of Democracy." American Journal of Chinese Studies 25, no. 2 (2018): 147–56.

3 See Zevelev, Igor. The Russian World in Moscow's Strategy. Washington, DC: Centre for Strategic & International Studies, August 22, 2016. https://www.csis.org/analysis/russian-world-moscows-strategy.

4 Quoted after Gronski, Aleksandr. "Russkii mir v poiskakh soderzhaniya." Rossiya v global'noi politike, Nr. 4 (August 24, 2017). https://globalaffairs.ru/articles/russkij-mir-v-poiskah-soderzhaniya/.

Spreading the ideology

The Russian state founded and used front organizations and transmission agencies abroad that organize public events, operate social media channels and exploit domestic frustrations, fears and emotional polarization as well as anti-liberal and anti-modernist sentiments. The ideology of the "Russian World" was spread abroad by organizations such as the "Russkii Mir Foundation", "Rossotrudnichestvo" (Russian Cooperation), "Russkoe Pole" (Russian Field) and the Russian Orthodox Church. In addition, the infrastructure of the "Congress of Russian Compatriots", through which the Russian authorities coordinate their influence abroad, has been successively expanded. In 2018, the Russian World Foundation and Rossotrudnichestvo signed an agreement to cooperate in promoting the Russian language and literature as well as the multinational culture of the Russian peoples. Furthermore, in 2007-2008, the Russian government initiated the distribution of a series of printed publications for the Russian diaspora as well as numerous online resources. Since 2007, Patriarch Kirill has been one of the trustees of the Russian World Foundation, which has centers and programs in at least 25 countries. The centers of the Russian World Foundation are also channels for Russian war propaganda, which is why the European Union imposed sanctions against the foundation in July 2022.

Orthodoxy and the "Russian world"

The leadership of the Russian Orthodox Church (ROC) under Metropolitan Kirill has adopted the diffuse concept of the "Russian World", which is particularly effective in its boldness. By joining the "Russian World" foundation in 2009, the ROC is also organizationally linked to its activities. Talk of the "Russian World" asserts a separate Russian civilization and the "spiritual" unity of a Russian Orthodox cultural area that transcends borders and peoples. The concept consists of a mixture of Russo-centric Slavophilia, statism, Great Russian ambitions, and Orthodox spatial policy.[5]

The borders of the "Russian world" are deliberately not defined; instead, a general claim is made to represent the Russian state and the Russian Orthodox Church for people who are influenced by the Russian language and culture. This is presented in a gesture of moral superiority over Western decadence and as a representation of true Christianity. The concept is collectivist, anti-enlightenment and directed against a secular understanding of the state.

The ROC sees itself as an ethical guideline for the "Russian world", to which legitimacy is thus ascribed. It sees itself as a pledge of unity to the "old Russian countries", by which it means Russia, Ukraine, and Belarus in particular. This provides an ideal superstructure for Putin's historical revanchism, for a retrofuture that seeks to subordinate the right to self-determination of the Slavic peoples of the Tsarist Empire and the Soviet Union to Russian supremacy.

The repeated talk of dark, hostile external powers, including the invocation of a battle against "Satanism", first by Metropolitan Kirill and then by Putin, reinforces the conflict over the scope of both Russian Orthodoxy and the Russian state. With its rhetoric of doom, its rhetorical revolt against modernity and its historical mythology, the ROC has made a decisive contribution to the radicalization of Putinism.

The ROC is at the center of the ideology of the "Russian world". Since 2007, Patriarch Kirill has repeatedly used the term, which he interprets as "a special civilization; and the people who belong to it today call themselves Russians, Ukrainians or Belarusians by different names." Therefore, Ukraine and Belarus also belong to "Holy Russia" or "Holy Rus", whether they like it or not. For the ROC, the political and administrative center of the "Russian

---

5 See Heinemann-Grüder, Andreas. Die Entmachtung der Gesellschaft durch die Russisch-Orthodoxe Kirche. Berlin: Konrad-Adenauer-Stiftung, January 2023. https://www.kas.de/documents/252038/22161843/Die+Entmachtung+der+Gesellschaft+durch+die+Russisch-Orthodoxe+Kirche.pdf.

world" is Moscow, while the spiritual center is ostensibly Kyiv.[6] According to Patriarch Kirill, the ROC should work with the Kremlin to promote spirituality, morality, and the unification of cultures.[7]

Immediately after the start of the war in February 2022, the ROC fully supported the aggression against Ukraine, while representatives of Christian churches around the world strongly opposed support for the war. The ROC portrayed the conflict as God being on the side of the God-believing Russian fighters, which then mutates the war into a divine right, even a form of worship service. The ROC is thus itself a party to the war.[8]

The ROC as a warring party

As early as 2014, pro-Russian separatism in the Donbass was supported by a "Russian Orthodox Army", which was subordinate to the "Oplot" battalion and is said to have comprised up to 4,000 combatants.[9] It is not known whether the ROC directly supported the "Russian Orthodox Army"; the Ukrainian Orthodox Church of the Moscow Patriarchate clearly distanced itself from the beginning. Nevertheless, the paramilitary force presented itself as a religious liberation army.

One of the most vocal media propagandists of the imperial takeover of Ukraine is Konstantin Malofeyev, the active religious-monarchist managing director of the investment fund Marshall Capital Partners. He is deputy chairman of the World Council of the Russian People, owner of the nationalist television channel

---

6 See Budraitskis, Ilya. "The Birth and Death of the 'Russian World': A History of the Concept." LeftEast, June 20, 2022. https://lefteast.org/the-birth-and-death-of-the-russian-world-a-history-of-the-concept/.

7 See Ukrainian Catholic Leader. "'Russian World' an Ideology Dressed in Church Vestments." Aleteia News, Oktober 23, 2022. https://aleteia.org/2022/10/23/ukrainian-catholic-leader-russian-world-an-ideology-dressed-in-church-vestments/.

8 As an overview see "Kak russkaja pravoslavnaja cerkov' podderživaet vojnu i čto delajut svjašennniki, s nej nesoglasnye," Novaja Gazeta, December 21, 2022, https://novayagazeta.ee/articles/2022/12/21/kak-russkaya-pravoslavnaya-tserkov-podderzhivaet-voinu-i-chto-delaiut-sviashchenniki-s-ney-neoglasnye.

9 See "Meet the Russian Orthodox Army, Ukrainian Separatists' Shock Troops." NBC News, May 16, 2014. https://www.nbcnews.com/storyline/ukraine-crisis/meet-russian-orthodox-army-ukrainian-separatists-shock-troops-n107326.

Tsargrad TV and head of a conspiracy theory institute called Katehon, as well as chairman of the board of the St. Basil the Great Foundation. Malofeyev provided extensive support for the separatists in Donbass during the so-called "Russian Spring" in 2014 and again from 2022 with his Orthodox liberation propaganda.[10]

The glorification of Russian warriors began with Patriarch Kirill long before the war in Ukraine. The expert on Eastern churches, Reinhard Flogaus, notes that Kirill had the principle of ecclesiastical education of the faithful "in the spirit of patriotism" enshrined in the church during his time as the second man of the Russian Orthodox Church. In this context, the "Social Doctrine" of the ROC from 2000, which he drafted, refers to the traditional ecclesiastical veneration of the Russian warrior princes of the Middle Ages and the duty of every believer to defend the Russian fatherland and their "blood brothers scattered across the world". Flogaus adds:

> "The narrative of `Holy Russia` serves Kiyrill as a pseudo-historical foundation for theological justification. Right at the beginning of the war, the patriarch sacralized Huntington's theory of a "clash of civilizations" and declared that Ukraine was about the question of salvation, about a metaphysical struggle for truth and against sin. According to the patriarch, the West wants to impose its sinful values on the people of Donbass and demands that they tolerate homosexuality and hold gay parades. This is incompatible with the values of Orthodoxy and the Russian world. That is why Russia must now come to the aid of its suffering fellow believers in Ukraine."[11]

When Putin announced a partial mobilization for the war against Ukraine in September 2022, Kirill asked his priests to pray for victory. The then 45-year-old Moscow priest Ioann Koval refused and

---

10 See Pilipenko, Evgen. "Na Donbas priechal rossijskij 'pravoslavnyj milliarder' — sonspor okupacii Malofeev." Liga.net, September 8, 2021. https://news.liga.net/politics/news/na-donbass-priehal-rossiyskiy-pravoslavnyy-milliarder-sponsor-okkupatsii-malofeev-foto; Jacinto, Leela. "God, Church, Tsar: The World of Russian Oligarch Malofeev and His Western Associates." France 24, April 8, 2022. https://www.france24.com/en/europe/20220408-god-church-tsar-the-world-of-russian-oligarch-malofeev-and-his-western-associates.

11 Rauch, Raphael. "Interview with Reinhard Flogaus: Der Brandbeschleuniger: Warum Patriarch Kyrill häretisch argumentiert." Kath.ch, December 6, 2022. https://www.kath.ch/newsd/der-brandstifter-warum-patriarch-kyrill-haeretisch-argumentiert/.

prayed for peace instead. Koval was dismissed. Of the approximately 40,000 priests of the ROC, only around 300 signed a letter calling for peace with Ukraine.[12]

The ROC collects "humanitarian aid" in its congregations abroad, including Germany, for victims of the war on the Russian side. A review of whether this is de facto support for the Russian occupying regime has not yet taken place.

According to the church leadership, priests who swap their Bible for the bayonet are considered loyal.[13] Instead of promoting Christian peace ethics, Metropolitan Kirill absolved the fighters against Ukraine at the end of September 2022, saying they would be cleansed of all previous sins. The war thus became a ritual of purification, where killing is no longer considered a sin, but a divine service.[14]

Implications

Kirill's policies have strengthened the centrifugal forces in the Russian Orthodox Church. On October 11, 2018, the Holy Synod of the Ecumenical Patriarchate of Constantinople revoked the right of the Patriarch of Moscow to ordain the Metropolitan of Kyiv. At the same time, all three Orthodox churches in Ukraine were placed under the Ecumenical Patriarchate in Constantinople (Istanbul). Since 2019, two Orthodox churches have existed side by side, the Ukrainian Orthodox Church of the Moscow Patriarchate under Metropolitan Onufriy and the Orthodox Church of Ukraine under Metropolitan Epiphanius.

---

12 See "Russian Orthodox Priests Persecuted for Supporting Peace in Ukraine." Associated Press, August 12, 2023. https://www.voanews.com/a/russian-orthodox-priests-persecuted-for-supporting-peace-in-ukraine-/7222972.html.
13 One church in southern Russia, for example, began teaching its Sunday school children how to fight unarmed and with bayonets, see Kilner, James. "Russian Children Swap Bibles for Bayonet Practice at Sunday School." The Telegraph, June 15, 2023. https://www.telegraph.co.uk/world-news/2023/06/15/russian-orthodox-church-children-bayonet-practice-ukraine/.
14 See Schmidt, Friedrich. Russlands Streitkräfte: Zu wenige wollen für Putin kämpfen. FAZ, September 5, 2022; "Patriarch of Moscow: Any Russian Soldier Who Dies in the War in Ukraine Is Forgiven for His Sins." Orthodox Times, September 26, 2022. https://orthodoxtimes.com/patriarch-of-moscow-any-russian-soldier-who-dies-in-the-war-in-ukraine-is-forgiven-for-his-sins/.

After the start of Russia's war, Metropolitan Onufrij called for the war to end immediately. The Ukrainian Orthodox Church, which was initially part of the Russian Orthodox Church, broke away from the Moscow Patriarchate on May 27, 2022. The Ukrainian Orthodox Church (Moscow Patriarchate) clearly distanced itself from Russia's war, but simultaneously it is still regarded by Ukrainian security agencies as a collaborator with the Kremlin. On December 2, 2022, Ukrainian President Zelensky introduced a bill into parliament to ban the Ukrainian Orthodox Church (Moscow Patriarchate), the law was adopted by the Ukrainian parliament on August 18, 2024.

Contrary to Kirill's intentions, his partisanship in the war has forced the Ukrainian Orthodox Church to break connections with Moscow, resulting in schism instead of unity. The ROC has also isolated itself from other Orthodox churches and Christian religious communities through its war policy. The leadership of the ROC is damaging itself by supporting Russia's war against Ukraine and thus is undermining its already weakened influence on the Orthodox faithful in Ukraine and in relation to the other Orthodox churches. The ROC's war propaganda only repels Orthodox believers outside Russia.

However, the ROC's influence could decline further if priests who oppose its leadership's course were supported, or if priests are called upon to speak out against the war. Some Russian Orthodox churches, such as those in the Baltic states, have declared their autocephaly, asserting independence from the Moscow Patriarchate, and others may follow suit.

In principle, the activities of Russian front organizations abroad require observation by the Federal Office for the Protection of the Constitution, the State Security Service, the Federal Intelligence Service, the media, and academic expertise. The ROC's propaganda for Russia's war is not covered by religious freedom. The ROC of the Moscow Patriarchate is part of Russia's "hybrid" warfare and should be treated as such.

The Russian Invasion and World Orthodoxy
A Geopolitical Schism?

Thomas Bremer

The Russian attack on Ukraine had a major impact on the religious situation in the country. But the war has also had consequences for Christian churches worldwide. This article will describe how Orthodoxy, the church to which most people in Ukraine belong, has been affected by the situation in Ukraine.

1 Prehistory

Orthodoxy is in the midst of a schism related to Ukraine. However, this did not arise with the war but had already begun in the fall of 2018. The Orthodox Church in Ukraine was divided; of the three larger churches, one was the Ukrainian branch of the Russian Orthodox Church (ROC), while the other two arose in connection with the collapse of the Soviet Union and Ukraine's independence. Until 2018, the latter two were considered uncanonical, i.e. they were not recognized by the other Orthodox churches in the world. The "Ukrainian Orthodox Church" (UOC), which was part of the Russian Church, was the only recognized legitimate Ukrainian church within Orthodoxy. This church was the largest, but the two non-canonical churches also had millions of believers and thousands of parishes, and they existed legally, according to Ukrainian religious legislation.

In the fall of 2018, the Ecumenical Patriarch of Constantinople, Bartholomew, set out to unite Orthodoxy in Ukraine and eliminate the existing irregular situation. He appointed two bishops as his envoys ("exarchs"), who organized a synod on his behalf in Kyiv on 15 December 2018, at which all Orthodox churches in the country were to unite. However, only the bishops of the two non-canonical churches attended this synod. They founded an "Orthodox Church of Ukraine" (OCU), which was recognized as autocephalous, i.e.

fully independent, by Patriarch Bartholomew a few weeks later. Instead of the previous three, there have now been two Orthodox churches since January 2019, both of which could consider themselves canonical – one due to its recognition by Constantinople, the other due to its connection with Moscow.

The ROC had protested Constantinople's actions from the outset. It regarded the territory of Ukraine as its own jurisdiction and forbade outside interference. Constantinople, in contrast, invoked the fact that Kyiv received Christianity from there in the 10th century; an act from 1686, in which the Ecumenical Patriarchate granted the Patriarch of Moscow certain prerogatives over the Kyiv Metropolis, was annulled by Constantinople in 2018.

The Patriarchate of Moscow reacted to the rehabilitation of the non-canonical bishops and the appointment of the exarchs by breaking off ecclesiastical relations. This is expressed above all by the fact that when the Moscow Patriarch celebrates the liturgy, he no longer mentions the name of the Patriarch of Constantinople in the prescribed place, but only the heads of the other Orthodox churches. Clergy of the Russian Church are forbidden to celebrate with those of Constantinople, and the Russian faithful are no longer allowed to receive the sacraments in the churches of the Ecumenical Patriarchate. Although the separation is not mutual, as Constantinople has not responded with the appropriate countermeasures, it does in fact mean that there has been an ongoing schism since 2018.

In Orthodoxy, who has the right to confer autocephaly on a newly established church is disputed – the Patriarchate of Constantinople as the first in the canonical order of the Orthodox Church, or the respective "mother church", i.e. the church to which the now independent church previously belonged. It is also disputed who is the "mother church" of Ukrainian Orthodoxy – Constantinople because of its foundation, or Moscow because Orthodoxy in Ukraine was administered from there for centuries. In any case, there is no clear answer to the question of the legitimacy of Bartholomew's actions. It should only be mentioned here that other factors also played a role – such as the boycott of the "Holy and Great Council of Orthodoxy" in 2016 by Moscow, and the political pressure from Kyiv.

2   Division of Orthodoxy

Since the fall of 2018, a schism has divided Moscow and Constantinople. Initially, other Orthodox churches remained neutral and did not take a clear position. However, over the next few months, three more churches (out of a total of around 14) recognized the OCU: the Church of Greece, the Patriarchate of Alexandria and the Church of Cyprus. The Russian Church reacted in the same way in all these cases, namely by breaking off communion. Only the Patriarchate of Alexandria reacted in the same way. This occurred when the Russian Church, after breaking off relations with Alexandria, set up its own ecclesiastical structures in Africa and persuaded several priests to move from Alexandria to Moscow's jurisdiction. These actions should also be seen in connection with Russian political ambitions in Africa.[1] Thus, a mutual schism has developed between Alexandria and Moscow.

In the Churches of Greece and Cyprus, the decision to recognize the OCU was controversial. Some of the bishops did not agree with this step but were outvoted by their colleagues. The Russian Church tried to exploit and deepen this division within the two churches. For instance, the Moscow Patriarchate published a list of Greek dioceses whose bishops had spoken out against recognition. Russian pilgrims should still be able to travel to these dioceses.

However, most other Orthodox churches remain in communion with both Constantinople and Moscow. Some have openly spoken out against recognition by Constantinople. For example, the widely recognized Archbishop of the Albanian Orthodox Church, Athanasios, has criticized Bartholomew's actions in a letter to him. In its announcements, the Serbian Church only refers to the head of the OCU by his surname ("Mr. Dumenko") because it does not recognize his episcopal dignity. The Serbian Patriarch Porfirije, who was elected in 2021, should have made inaugural visits to the other Orthodox churches, in canonical order – but as he apparently does

---

1   A few months after the death of the Russian mercenary leader Prigozhin, whose "Wagner" formation is present in Africa, Metropolitan Leonid, who was apparently closely associated with Prigozhin and responsible for Africa, was first withdrawn from Africa and then retired at the age of 55.

not want to meet Patriarch Bartholomew in the current situation, Porfirije has now been to North and South America and various European countries, but not to traditional Orthodox states (with the exception of a short visit to Russia for a funeral).

Other churches indicate their stance by concelebrating with hierarchs of the UOC, but not with those of the OCU. In addition to the Serbian church, this applies to the churches of Romania, Poland, and the one of the Czech Republic and Slovakia.

There have been several attempts and appeals from other Orthodox churches to clarify the situation. In February 2020, the Patriarch of Jerusalem invited the heads of all recognized Orthodox churches to a dialogue. While the Russian church and five others attended the meeting, Patriarch Bartholomew canceled in advance, arguing that only he had the right to convene such a meeting. Later, Bartholomew refused to discuss his decision regarding Ukraine because the issue had been definitively resolved.

3 Reactions to the war

It should be noted that the split in Orthodoxy was not caused by the Russian attack on Ukraine but had already existed beforehand. The frontline position between the first patriarchate according to canonical ranking, Constantinople, and the numerically largest, Moscow, which became apparent in the disputes over Ukrainian autocephaly, is also evident in the reactions to the war: Russian Patriarch Kirill famously justified the Russian attack on Ukraine, portraying it as a defensive struggle against the collective West, which wanted to impose its way of life on Ukraine.[2] Kirill's view is very much in line with the arguments of the Russian government. When accused of supporting the war, representatives of the Russian church usually respond by saying that the church prays for peace and that it stays out of politics. As prayer for peace is part of every Orthodox service, it is nothing new. However, Patriarch Kirill decreed in September 2022 that a prayer for Russia's victory should be said in the church services.

---

[2] See Willems, Joachim. "Ein Diener zweier Herren. Patriarch Kirill und seine Kriegspredigten." Osteuropa 73 (2023): 221–34.

Patriarch Bartholomew of Constantinople has condemned the war in no uncertain terms. In an interview shortly after the invasion, he defended his decision to grant the OCU autocephaly as a correct and timely act.[3] In a later statement, he regretted that no condemnation of the war came from Patriarch Kirill: "It is not possible for the churches not to condemn violence and war. But the Church of Russia has let us down."[4] The Orthodox Church of Finland, which enjoys autonomy within the Ecumenical Patriarchate, also condemned both the war and the attitude of the Russian Church.[5] The other Orthodox churches also regretted the war in the first days and weeks, but initially held back with political assessments.[6] It is remarkable that the statements often refer to their own experiences of war — the Patriarchate of Jerusalem mentions the difficult situation of the Palestinians, the Serbian Church mentions Kosovo and the Georgian Church refers to the conflict over Abkhazia. In many of the critical statements, the West is accused of double standards because it does not care about these conflicts, but sees the war in Ukraine, which it allegedly provoked itself, as a major and particular problem.

In principle, the camps that emerged in the dispute over Orthodoxy in Ukraine are also reflected in the assessment of the war. Clear apportionment of blame is avoided. However, the Serbian Orthodox Church, like the Patriarchate of Jerusalem, sees the West as the culprit, while the Romanian Church was quick to name Russia as the aggressor. In his Epiphany address in 2024, the then Bulgarian Patriarch sided surprisingly clearly with Ukraine.[7] His successor, however, is regarded as a Russophile. The churches in EU

---

3   See Orthodoxie aktuell: Informationen aus der Orthodoxen Kirche. 3-4 (2022), 8. The monthly magazine "Orthodoxie Aktuell", published by the Orthodox Bishops' Conference in Germany, offers reliable documentation of the events and statements of the various Orthodox churches.
4   Orthodoxie aktuell: Informationen aus der Orthodoxen Kirche. 6 (2022), 7.
5   See Orthodoxie aktuell: Informationen aus der Orthodoxen Kirche. 3-4 (2022)
6   See Orthodoxie aktuell 3-4, 11-12.
7   See Atanassov, Vladislav. "Bulgarien: Patriarchat kritisiert Krieg gegen die Ukraine deutlich". January 2024. https://noek.info/nachrichten/suedosteuropa/33-bulgarien/3189-bulgarien-patriarch-kritisiert-krieg-gegen-die-ukraine-deutlich.

states with an Orthodox majority (Greece, Cyprus, Romania, Bulgaria) are mostly critical of Russia, majority churches in non-EU states (Serbia, Georgia) tend to criticize the West, while the old patriarchates (Alexandria, Antioch, Jerusalem) and the minority churches (Poland, Czech lands and Slovakia, Albania) take different positions. This division is not geopolitical in the classical sense but depends on many different factors.

Nevertheless, it must be pointed out that almost all Orthodox churches are still in communion with each other while Russia has unilaterally broken communion with four churches, and the only complete schism is between Moscow and Alexandria. Despite this, all other churches remain in communion with both Moscow and Alexandria, even if this contradicts canonical logic. Patriarch Bartholomew of Constantinople commemorates the heads of all other churches during celebrations including Patriarch Kirill. Thus, the division within Orthodoxy is real, but has so far had very few cases with significant canonical consequences.

4 Final Consideration

The current schism in Orthodoxy highlights that tensions and fundamental differences existed long before the Ecumenical Patriarchate's decision to grant autocephaly to the OCU, but that these tensions remained largely unnoticed.[8] The Russian boycott of the 2016 All-Orthodox Council was a clear sign of this opposition. It would be valuable to trace these differences theologically to understand the ecclesiological approaches underlying the two positions.

The crisis also shows that Orthodoxy lacks the necessary instruments to make decisions that are accepted by all churches. It is widely known that the last ecumenical council recognized by world Orthodoxy was more than 1,200 years ago. While there appear to be fewer problems and frictions in dogmatic questions than in issues of church organization, even the two competing churches in Ukraine do not differ from each other dogmatically (and almost not

---

8   See Bremer, Thomas, Alfons Brüning, und Nadieszda Kizenko, Hrsg. Orthodoxy in Two Manifestations? The Conflict in Ukraine as Expression of a Fault Line in World Orthodoxy. Berlin, 2022.

liturgically). Nonetheless, they do dispute each other's canonicity. As we have seen, there is no consensus on this question among other churches either, nor is there a mechanism to resolve it. Regular meetings of the first hierarchs, such as those held in preparation for the Council of 2016, and conciliar mechanisms, for which this Council could be a starting point, could help clarify or avoid similar situations in the future. Currently, it is not foreseeable that there will be any movement on the specific issue of Ukrainian church organization or even on the fundamental question of ways of reaching agreement within Orthodoxy. Consequently, it is to be feared that the current division will continue for a very long time.

Jewish Life in Russia and Ukraine
A Paradigm Shift Since the Invasion?

Pinchas Goldschmidt

In retrospect, February 24, 2022, the day of the Russian attack on the entire territory of Ukraine, could be the day that sealed the end of the renaissance of Jewry in Russia. This was a community that had existed in its form for just over 30 years and that was established with great effort after the fall of communism and the end of the Soviet Union, in which Jewish life was largely suppressed.

I personally had been working as a rabbi in Moscow since 1989. February 24, 2022, clarified that I could no longer stay in the country.

Although the signs were visible, nobody wanted to admit in February 2022 that everything would deteriorate for the Russian Jewish community. The invasion of Ukraine transformed Russia from an authoritarian to a semi-totalitarian system virtually overnight. Opposition members were arrested by the thousands. The last remnants of free media were silenced, such as the radio station "Ekho Moskvy" or the newspaper "Novaya Gazeta". The internet has been censored, and journalists and those running non-governmental organisations were declared foreign agents. The country's last liberal politicians were shown the door.

Jewish opposition figures, including Putin critic Vladimir Kara-Murza and former party leader Leonid Gosman, were particularly targeted by the Putin regime. The Kremlin demanded unconditional obedience to its course in Ukraine from the country's religious communities. I was also put on the list of "foreign agents" in June 2022, along with other members of civil society.[1]

The anti-Semitism that was always present in Russia was also stoked by the regime. Foreign Minister Sergey Lavrov claimed

---

[1] See Toi staff und AP. "Russia Brands Exiled Former Moscow Chief Rabbi a 'Foreign Agent.'" Times of Israel, July 2, 2022. https://www.timesofisrael.com/russia-brands-exiled-former-moscow-chief-rabbi-a-foreign-agent/.

about the Jewish President of Ukraine, Volodymyr Zelensky, that as history had shown, the most ardent anti-Semites were usually the Jews themselves.[2]

Shortly after the start of the "special military operation" against Ukraine, the presidential administration and the FSB domestic intelligence service called on the country's rabbis to sign a declaration condemning the "Nazi regime in Kyiv" and expressing their support for the Russian war. It was clear to everyone that refusal to do so would result in severe penalties.

Furthermore, Vladimir Putin passed a law making the use of the word "war" a punishable offence. After 33 years in Moscow and almost three decades as chief rabbi in the capital, I decided to leave the country. I asked myself some questions: Would I abandon the community I had served for so long by leaving?

The answer was very clear: In contrast to earlier times, when Jews could not leave the country or could do so only with great difficulty, it was now possible to leave. I was not the only one to turn my back on Russia. Around 100,000 Russian Jews have left the country since the outset of the war, with 38,000 emigrating to Israel in the months following the invasion alone. In other words, more than a third of Russia's Jewish population has fled—an enormous bloodletting for the communities there.

This was certainly not the first wave of emigration. Many Jews had already left the countries of the Soviet Union in the 1990s. Yet simultaneously, many had stayed, professed their Judaism, or rediscovered it. New synagogues were built, Jewish festivals celebrated, and new communities founded, especially in the big cities like Moscow.

However, these communities were primarily financed by a few oligarchs, many of them Jewish and generous, who had become very wealthy under Boris Yeltsin in the 1990s. When Vladimir Putin replaced Boris Yeltsin as president at the turn of the millennium, some of the oligarchs became a thorn in the side of the new strongman because they were not afraid to criticize Putin. One example is

---

2 See ORF. "Lawrow sorgt mit Nazi-Vergleich für Empörung." ORF, Israel, May 2, 2022. https://orf.at/stories/3263192/.

Vladimir Gussinsky, whom Putin quickly identified as one of his enemies. At the end of the 1990s, Gussinsky had helped to build up Jewish life in Russia with his generous donations. From 1996 to 2000, he was president of the umbrella organization Russian-Jewish Congress.

Gussinsky falling out of favor negatively impacted the community, as the Kremlin deliberately promoted a separate structure led by the rabbi of the Chabad-Lubavitch movement, Berel Lazar, who was loyal to the regime. Lazar became what would previously have been called a "court Jew" at Putin's court. He was given the title "Putin's rabbi" for a reason, and he had no problem with it: Lazar never publicly criticizes the Kremlin. He has Putin's ear. But conversely, he is also the Kremlin's mouthpiece — internationally and towards the Jewish community.[3] Although Lazar calls himself "Chief Rabbi of the Russian Federation", he only represents a minority of Jews in the country.

His actions over the last 20 years have contributed to an overly rosy view of the situation of Jews in Russia being spread around the world. Only a few years ago, one could read in the Western media that antisemitism had supposedly been defeated. Jewish leaders also parroted this. But all that glittered was not gold. This became clear to everyone at the latest with the war against Ukraine. The overwhelming majority of Russian Jews are against this war.

When I left Moscow at the beginning of March 2022 to go into exile, there was a discussion about who should succeed me as Moscow's chief rabbi. The head of a small community in the capital, Schlomo Zlotsky, was initially the only candidate acceptable to the authorities, as KEROOR, the Central Council of Religious Jewish Communities, had refused to support the "special operation". Therefore, the Russian government and the FSB secret service decided to pursue Zlotsky's appointment as chief rabbi of Moscow. In return, Zlotsky was supposed to support the Ukraine campaign publicly. He did so and appeared on a state television station,

---

3 See Klein, Zvivka. "Russian Chief Rabbi Lazar Addresses Putin: 'No Peace with Terrorists.'" Jerusalem Post, October 27, 2023. https://www.jpost.com/international/islamic-terrorism/article-770387.

where he made a very obscure statement. He was one of the few Jewish community leaders to bless Putin's war.

The Chief Rabbinate in Israel was very worried about the developments in Moscow. It issued a letter stating that it would continue to regard me as Chief Rabbi and head of the Beit Din, the rabbinical court. The community, which was responsible for electing the rabbi, was also concerned. At a meeting, I was re-elected for another seven years in absentia. Given the circumstances, it was a rather symbolic election and a way for the Jewish community to express its disapproval of the regime. Had this not happened, the FSB would probably have spread the story that Pinchas Goldschmidt had to leave due to a lack of popularity or even because of a scandal. But the authorities were not prepared to accept the matter simply. I received a formal letter from Chief Rabbi Adolf Shayevich stating that my contract would not be extended.

In early summer 2022, I gave an interview[4] to the Jewish magazine *Mishpacha* and explained for the first time why I would not return to Russia under Putin. The article was translated into Russian. A few days later, the FSB visited the leadership of the Moscow Jewish community and demanded that my contract be terminated. Realizing that holding on to my position would endanger my community, I resigned as the Chief Rabbi of Moscow.

Relations between Russia and Israel also deteriorated during the war. When Israeli politicians rebuked Moscow for the invasion of Ukraine, the Kremlin decided to retaliate. The victim of this retaliation was the Jewish Agency for Israel, which is responsible worldwide for aliyah, the immigration of Jews from the diaspora to Israel.[5] Although the Jewish Agency is no longer necessary for the emigration process, as the administrative part is handled by the Israeli embassy in the respective country, its support in relocation and integration is of central importance. The Russian Ministry of

---

4 See Guttentag, Gedalia. "Do Svidaniya, Russia." Mishpacha Magazine, July 5, 2022. https://mishpacha.com/do-svidaniya-russia/.

5 See Reuters. "Russia Moves to Dissolve Jewish Agency Branch That Promotes Immigration to Israel." Reuters, July 21, 2022. https://www.reuters.com/world/europe/russian-justice-ministry-asks-jewish-agency-be-dissolved-2022-07-21/.

Justice sent the Jewish Agency a letter announcing the withdrawal of its accreditation. The official complaint was that the collection of personal data of Russian citizens (in this case Jewish citizens) on servers outside Russia was unlawful. The real reason, however, was the Israeli government's statements on the war in Ukraine. Additionally, there was a desire to prevent the emigration of skilled workers, as the departure of mostly well-educated Jews represented a significant economic loss for Russia.

Jewish associations in Russia called on the country's Jews to stay, but they voted with their feet. Living in Russia had become impossible with the invasion of Ukraine. A Jewish life under Putin, whom some Jewish leaders from the West were still praising a few years ago for successfully combating anti-Semitism, does not seem possible in the foreseeable future.

In 2022, the former dissident Natan Sharansky, perhaps the Soviet Union's best-known "Prisoner of Zion", called on all Jews in Russia to leave the country immediately. He has good reasons. Of course, no one has a crystal ball. No one knows what the future will bring for Russia and Russian Jews. But as long as Vladimir Putin is at the helm, there is no hope of Jewish life flourishing again in the country.

What about Ukraine? After the end of the Soviet Union, it was a place too where Jewish communities were founded. Jewish life flourished again in Kyiv, Odessa, and many other cities. In addition to parallels with Russia—one similarity is the financing by oligarchs—there are also differences. The most visible one being that Jewish politicians in Ukraine were able to succeed despite their Jewishness. Ukraine has already had a Jewish prime minister, and in Volodymyr Zelensky it even has a Jewish president of whom many in the country are proud. A Jewish politician holding a senior government position would be unthinkable in Putin's Russia nowadays.

Many Jews also fled Ukraine during the war. However—and this is remarkable—they were fewer in number than Jews from Russia. It has also been shown that Ukrainian Jews predominantly identify with their country's political system. The experience of the war has reinforced this. While there was still some sympathy with

Russia and warnings of Jew-hatred among the nationalist forces in Ukraine before February 2022, this has since faded.

The situation is very different in Russia. Many of the remaining Jews there are in what could be called "inner emigration". With the exception of the so-called "oligarchs", very few Russian Jews nowadays sympathize with the Kremlin ruler or openly show such affection.

The narrative that a regime of "neo-Nazis" is at work in Kyiv does not resonate with Russian Jews. False claims such as Foreign Minister Lavrov's, namely that the worst antisemites are the Jews themselves, are seen for what they are: calculated insults that use anti-Semitic resentment to stir up public opinion for a war that has by no means produced the results that were hoped for.

Looking back at Russian history, regimes have always tried to direct the anger of the masses towards the Jewish community when the political system was in danger. Jews have been a convenient scapegoat for governments of all stripes, from the tsars to Stalin to Putin. This is the case again today. Nonetheless, a lot of reconstruction work has been done in the last three decades. However, everyone was always aware that it was a dance on a powder keg.

For the foreseeable future, Russia will not be a good place for Jews. But the same would have been said about Germany after 1945. As we all know, things turned out somewhat differently. I will not give up hope for a better future.

Papal Diplomacy for Ukraine
Naïve Pacifism or Strategic Neutrality?

Ludwig Ring-Eifel

The Pope's non-partisan position

Pope Francis' positions on the Russian-Ukrainian war have repeatedly led to irritation. Unlike under John Paul II (1978-2005), this time the Holy See is not acting as an ideal ally of "the West" in an East-West conflict but is seeking a role *supra partes*. One reason for this is of an ideological nature: the Cold War against the Soviet Union and its vassal states was also a struggle of the "Free World" (which guaranteed religious freedom) against a totalitarian and largely atheistic system. This time, the aggressive Empire in the East is acting as a self-proclaimed "defender of traditional Christian values" and in harmony with the Russian Orthodox Church, which is an important ecumenical interlocutor for the Pope. For the Vatican, Putin's Russia — in contrast to the Soviet Union in the past — is not an ideological opponent. Pope Francis is, therefore, not joining the phalanx of Western (liberal) states that oppose Putin. Rather, he is seeking a superior position as the "advocate of all humanity". This is based on one optimistic and one pessimistically motivated pacifist conviction. On the one hand, he clings to the vision of world peace formulated in the 2020 encyclical "Fratelli tutti", which — he believes — can and must be achieved in the face of global challenges such as climate change.[1] On the other hand, there is the Pope's warning of a "Third World War in pieces", which he sees escalating dramatically in the Russian-Ukrainian war. From the lofty vantage point of a visionary of world peace and at the same time a doomsday prophet of world war, the Pope sees himself in the role of a possible mediator and acts in a correspondingly neutral manner. He calls for respect for international law, demands compliance with

---

[1] See Franziskus. Enzyklika Fratelli tutti (October 3, 2020). Acta Apostolicae Sedis 112 (2020), chapters 35f., 127 and 137 f.

humanitarian standards, and condemns the madness of war itself. However, he largely ignores the question of who the aggressor in this war is and even questions the Western narrative of Russia's sole responsibility.

In doing so, the Pope is imitating Benedict XV's (failed) attempt to mediate between Germany and France during the First World War (1914-1918). Even then, the Pope was almost alone in his view that not only one side (the German Reich) was to blame for the war. Pope Francis' basic attitude towards war as an "insane" event that only knows losers apart from the arms manufacturers was probably significantly influenced by his Italian grandfather, whose experiences in the First World War Francis reported on anecdotally in interviews.[2]

Added to this is the fundamental questioning of the Church's doctrine of a just (i.e. defensive) war, which was already formulated in the encyclical Fratelli Tutti (2020). There, Francis wrote: "We can no longer think of war as a solution, because its risks will probably always be greater than its supposed benefits. In view of this, it is very difficult nowadays to invoke the rational criteria elaborated in earlier centuries to speak of the possibility of a "just war". Never again war!"[3]

The Vatican has repeatedly tried to condemn the war and contribute to peace without unilaterally blaming Russia. It has been doing so since this war began in 2014 with the annexation of Crimea.

Communication channels of the Holy See during the war

Hardly any other figure of global importance has addressed this war as often as Pope Francis. He uses a wide variety of communication channels to exert his influence, for instance, in public speeches on St. Peter's Square, in messages for the World Day of

---

2 Piqué, Elisabetta. "Entrevista de LA NACION con el papa Francisco: 'Quiero ir a Kyiv, pero con la condición de ir también a Moscú.'" March 11, 2023. https://www.lanacion.com.ar/el-mundo/entrevista-de-la-nacion-con-el-papa-francisco-quiero-ir-a-kiev-pero-con-la-condicion-de-ir-tambien-a-nid11032023/.
3 Fratelli tutti, 258.

Peace, and in New Year's addresses to ambassadors accredited to the Holy See, as well as in numerous interviews and press conferences.

In addition to the Pope, Cardinal Secretary of State Pietro Parolin and the "Vatican Foreign Affairs Minister", Archbishop Paul Gallagher from Great Britain, also make public statements, even if they are rather rare. There are also the nuncios in Kyiv and Moscow, who usually work discreetly. As Parolin and Gallagher are professional diplomats, their statements sometimes differ from those of the Pope in their choice of words and style. As a religious leader, Francis often speaks in terms that do not correspond to the rules of international politics. Furthermore, there are sometimes differences in content between the Pope and his foreign policy staff.

Francis also uses other channels for his peace efforts. In the first weeks of the war, he sent Cardinals Konrad Krajewski and Michael Czerny to Ukraine on humanitarian missions, which was primarily a symbolic presence. In the words of the Pope: "The presence of the two cardinals there is not only the presence of the Pope, but that of the entire Christian people, who show their closeness and say: 'The war is madness! Please stop it! Look at this cruelty!'"[4] Even on this occasion, the Pope said: "The Holy See is ready to do everything to put itself at the service of peace." This sentence soon triggered speculation that he might be prepared to travel personally to Kyiv and Moscow to work for peace. However, such a trip never took place. In an interview with the Argentine newspaper *La Nación*, he explained that he had set the conditions for a peace mission so high that it was almost impossible to achieve. Unlike Western politicians who demonstrated their solidarity with Ukraine in Kyiv or Butscha, the Pope argued that he could only travel to Kyiv if he also visited Moscow — a dream that the popes before him had never been able to realize even under simpler foreign policy circumstances. On this occasion, Francis praised President Putin

---

4 Pope Francis. "Le parole del Papa alla recita dell' Angelus." March 6, 2022. https://press.vatican.va/content/salastampa/it/bollettino/pubblico/2022/03/06/0160/00340.html.

(more than a year after the start of the invasion) as an "educated man with whom you can hold high-level talks".[5]

Two months after the interview and a week after a meeting with Ukrainian President Zelenskyy in the Vatican, Francis opened another channel of communication, a kind of "parallel humanitarian diplomacy". He commissioned the President of the Italian Bishops' Conference, Cardinal Matteo Zuppi, with a vaguely defined "peace mission". Vatican press spokesman Matteo Bruni described the mission on May 20, 2023, as follows:

> "Pope Francis has entrusted Cardinal Matteo Zuppi, Archbishop of Bologna and President of the Italian Bishops' Conference, with the responsibility of leading a mission, in agreement with the Secretariat of State, that contributes to an easing of tensions in the Ukraine conflict, in the hopes that this can initiate paths of peace, something never abandoned by the Holy Father."[6]

Since then, Zuppi has met high-ranking interlocutors in Washington, Kyiv, Moscow, and Beijing, but his statements on a possible peace solution have remained vague. Recently, Zuppi has further lowered expectations of the mission, saying that only humanitarian mediation in the exchange of prisoners of war and the return of minors to Ukraine was expected.

Moreover, Pope Francis engages primarily with religious communities, with his Russian counterpart being the Moscow Patriarch Cyril. In keeping with Orthodox tradition, the head of the world's largest Orthodox church is very close to the ruler of his state. This is another reason why it is instructive to take a closer look at the Pope's communication with the Patriarch about Ukraine.

Vatican statements on the war from 2014 to 2024

Since the outcomes of Vatican diplomacy in this war can hardly be measured, this analysis is limited to what the Pope and his diplomatic and para-diplomatic actors have said publicly.

---

5   Piqué, 2023.
6   "Pope entrusts Cardinal Zuppi with Ukraine peace mission" May 20, 2023. https://www.vaticannews.va/en/pope/news/2023-05/pope-entrusts-cardinal-zuppi-with-ukraine-peace-mission.html.

One of the Pope's first public statements was published two days after the signing of the Minsk Agreement on September 5, 2014, which was intended to pacify the skirmishes in Eastern Ukraine that, at the time were still regarded as a regional separatist conflict. The Pope described the agreement as a "significant step in the search for a ceasefire in the regions affected by the conflict in eastern Ukraine."[7] He hoped that this could contribute to "efforts to achieve lasting peace."[8]

The Holy See had also not publicly rebuked the annexation of Crimea in March 2014. Two years later, Francis became the first pope in church history to meet the head of the Russian Orthodox Church. The event took place on February 12, 2016, at Havana airport. The ecclesiastical summit between "Rome" and "Moscow" was a diplomatic and religious-political success for the Pope. But the price was high. Francis agreed to a joint declaration that many Ukrainians found offensive. In the text, Putin's hybrid war, which had been festering for two years, was described as a "conflict in Ukraine". The fact that Russia was behind it was not mentioned. The statement read:

> "We deplore the hostility in Ukraine that has already caused many victims, inflicted innumerable wounds on peaceful inhabitants and thrown society into a deep economic and humanitarian crisis. We invite all the parts involved in the conflict to prudence, to social solidarity and to action aimed at constructing peace. We invite our Churches in Ukraine to work towards social harmony, to refrain from taking part in the confrontation, and to not support any further development of the conflict."[9]

Cyril flew to Cuba for the meeting on Putin's presidential plane. The huge Ilyushin Il-96-300-PU with the inscription "Rossiya" formed the visual backdrop for the ceremony, which was accompanied by hugs and pleasantries. On the Ukrainian side, the Havana

---

7   Pope Francis. "Le parole del Papa alla recita dell' Angelus." September 7, 2014. https://press.vatican.va/content/salastampa/it/bollettino/pubblico/2014/09/07/0615/01366.html.

8   Ibid.

9   "Meeting of his Holiness Pope Francis with his Holiness Kirill, Patriarch of Moscow and all Russia. Signing of the Joint Declaration." February 12, 2016. https://www.vatican.va/content/francesco/en/speeches/2016/february/documents/papa-francesco_20160212_dichiarazione-comune-kirill.html.

declaration was sharply criticized. The spiritual leader of the Greek-Catholic minority in Ukraine, Grand Archbishop Sviatoslav Shevchuk, reported in an interview that many Ukrainians felt "disappointed and betrayed by Rome". The Pope responded to this in a press conference and that he sees his role in the conflict as a *supra partes* speaking to the Russian and Ukrainian presidents with the conclusion that there are different opinions about what a war is and who started it.¹⁰

Six years later, when the hybrid war in Donbass turned into open military aggression by Russia, the Pope used similar terminology. On the day before the Russian invasion, Francis did not take sides with Ukraine, but made himself the spokesman for humanity during the Angelus prayer, saying: "Like me, many people around the world feel fear and concern. Once again, the peace of all is threatened by individual interests [...] I ask all parties involved to refrain from actions that bring even more suffering to the population, destabilize coexistence and discredit international law."¹¹

The day after the attack, Cardinal Parolin also chose impartial formulations that described the conflict from a quasi-planetary perspective. He repeated the Pope's appeal from the previous day and explained: "This appeal takes on a dramatic urgency after the start of Russia's military operations on the territory of Ukraine." Nevertheless, "there remains room for negotiations and for acting wisely, preventing individual interests from prevailing, protecting the legitimate aspirations of all and sparing the world the madness and horrors of war."¹²

Parolin spoke—more specifically—of "Russian military operations on the territory of Ukraine" and no longer just of a "conflict

---

10 See "Pressekonferenz von Papst Franziskus auf dem Rückflug nach Rom." February 18, 2016. https://press.vatican.va/content/salastampa/it/bollettino/pubblico/2016/02/18/0136/00288.html.
11 "L'Udienza Generale." February 23, 2022. https://press.vatican.va/content/salastampa/it/bollettino/pubblico/2022/02/23/0131/00273.html.
12 "Dichiarazione del Cardinale Segretario di Stato Pietro Parolin." February 24, 2022. https://press.vatican.va/content/salastampa/it/bollettino/pubblico/2022/02/24/0137/00298.html.

in Ukraine". Nevertheless, he did not deviate from the Pope's diction and did not use terms such as aggression or (legitimate) defense.

In the first weeks of the war, Pope Francis used every other public address to evoke the horrors of war in ever more dramatic terms. He condemned "the belligerents" or "the diabolical and perverse logic of weapons". It was a month before he uttered the word "invasion" on February 27, 2022, at the Angelus prayer. The Pope said: "More than a month has passed since the beginning of the invasion of Ukraine, since the beginning of this cruel and senseless war, which, like every war, means a defeat for all people."[13]

Once again, the Pope did not name Russia as the aggressor and did not mention the legitimate right of the attacked state to self-defense. Instead, he stepped up his condemnation of the war itself, which he described as "bestiality" and a "barbaric and blasphemous act".

Two months later, when the Russian invaders had conquered large portions of southern Ukraine, the Pope appeared largely helpless and at a loss in an interview with the "Corriere della Sera". He mentioned that his relationship with Patriarch Cyril had been severed after the Pope had accused him in a video conference of acting as a "state cleric" for Putin. Furthermore, despite a request from the Cardinal Secretary of State in Moscow, Putin had also refused to meet with the Pope. Meanwhile, Russia was advancing further. In this conversation, from which the newspaper only published individual quotes, the Pope attempted to explain Putin's behavior for the first time. He suggested that perhaps it was the "barking of NATO at the gates of Russia" that provoked Putin, arguing that Nato's actions might have been, if not the direct cause, then at least a factor that "encouraged" Putin's "anger".[14]

---

13   "Dichiarazione del Cardinale Segretario di Stato Pietro Parolin." February 27, 2022. https://press.vatican.va/content/salastampa/it/bollettino/pubblico/2022/02/24/0137/00298.html.
14   Fontana, Luciano. "Intervista a Papa Francesco: 'Putin non si ferma, voglio incontrarlo a Mosca. Ora non vado a Kiev.'" May 4, 2022. https://www.corriere.it/cronache/22_maggio_03/intervista-papa-francesco-putin-694c35f0-ca57-11ec-829f-386f144a5eff.shtml.

The Pope's comments caused disgruntlement in the West. Ten days later, Foreign Minister Gallagher spoke in a television interview with RAI for the first time, apparently to calm the waters after the Pope's interview. He stated that Ukraine had a right to self-defense and that arms deliveries to the invaded country were justified.[15]

The Pope's expression of the "madness of war", prevailing on both sides, six months after the invasion, almost led to a diplomatic scandal. The Ukrainian ambassador Andrij Jurasch, who was present at the speech, told the Catholic News Agency (CNA) immediately afterward that it was "not appropriate to put Ukraine and Russia on the same level in this situation". It was not Ukraine that had attacked Russia, but thousands of Russian soldiers who had murdered innocent Ukrainian civilians. Finally, the Secretariat of State of the Holy See resorted to an unusual means. On August 30, 2022, it published a statement in which it corrected the Pope's statements:

> "There has been a public debate about the political significance to be attributed to these statements. In this regard, it should be emphasized that the Holy Father's words in this drama are to be understood as a voice in defense of human life [...] and not as political statements. Considering the extensive war in Ukraine launched by the Russian Federation, the statements of the Holy Father Francis are clear and unambiguous: they condemn this war as morally unjustified, unacceptable, barbaric, senseless, repugnant and blasphemous."[16]

Three weeks later, at a press conference on his return flight from Kazakhstan, the Pope spoke in general terms about the fact that even a country under attack has a moral right to self-defense.[17]

The Pope continued to express new appeals for the "tormented Ukrainian people" in the following months of war. Meanwhile, his

---

15 See Ceraso, Gabriella, "Archbishop Gallagher: Ukraine has right to defend itself but beware arms race" May 13, 2022. https://www.vaticannews.va/en/vatican-city/news/2022-05/abp-gallagher-ukraine-has-the-right-to-defend-itself.html

16 "Communicato della Santa Sede." August 30, 2022. https://press.vatican.va/content/salastampa/it/bollettino/pubblico/2022/08/30/0627/01269.html.

17 See "Press Conference on the Return Flight to Rome." September 15, 2022. https://www.vatican.va/content/francesco/en/speeches/2022/september/documents/20220915-kazakhstan-voloritorno.html.

diplomats and his peace envoy, Cardinal Mateo Zuppi, were looking for "humanitarian ways to overcome hatred" and were successfully involved in the repatriation of abducted Ukrainian children and the exchange of prisoners of war.

At the beginning of March 2024, the Pope caused a worldwide stir when he said in a Swiss television interview: "I believe that the stronger person is the one who understands the situation, who thinks of the population, who has the courage to raise the white flag, to negotiate."[18] After that, he emphasized: "Negotiation is never surrender. It is the courage not to lead the country to suicide."[19]

Thereby, the Pope went beyond the general condemnation of the war and made a pragmatic advance that was widely understood as advice to Ukraine, which was structurally inferior in the war. Once again, many people, from the press spokesman to the nuncio in Kyiv, had to step in to clarify the Pope's words and defend him against a wave of indignation surging throughout the West.

The Italian historian Andrea Riccardi, founder of the Community of Sant'Egidio, clarified in this debate that the Pope's pacifist position in this war could also be a realistic one. He argued that Ukraine was at a crossroads. The alternatives are "the defeat of Ukraine or its gradual bleeding to death in an even bigger war"[20].

Since the deployment of Western troops in Ukraine is no longer ruled out, the Pope has once again stepped up his rhetoric, warning of a world war in his Easter 2024 address:

---

18 Sacharowa, Maria. "Papst irritiert mit Aussagen zum Ukrainekrieg." March 11, 2024. https://www.srf.ch/play/tv/srf-news-videos/video/papst-irritiert-mit-aussagen-zum-ukrainekrieg?urn=urn:srf:video:a8d01af8-7b41-4061-a607-4eb5ee2ff8a9.
19 Ibid.
20 "Zelenski dopo le parole del Papa: nessuna resa, la Chiesa è al fronte" March 11, 2024. https://archivio.corriere.it/Archivio/interface/slider.html#!riccardi/11-03-2024/11-03-2024/NobwRAdghgtgpmAXGAJlALlMAaMAzAJwHsYkwBGcgegAYBmKgJhsYBYcx0izLaHm2YAL7Zw0eGQDWcAJ4B3IgRQd0cAB7oyBAJYBjXVCXbhAXSA.

"Let us not allow the strengthening winds of war to blow on Europe and the Mediterranean. Let us not yield to the logic of weapons and rearming. Peace is never made with arms, but with outstretched hands and open hearts"[21].

Apparently, the longer the war lasts and the further it spreads, the more Pope Francis sees his pacifist stance confirmed. However, the Pope's decision, which has been maintained since the beginning of the conflict, not to name and condemn the aggressor in this war, remains highly problematic and threatens to undermine the moral authority of this pacifist Pope. It was all the more surprising that Zelenskyy and his ambassador Jurash changed their wording regarding the Vatican considerably after the president had been to the Vatican for a third time on October 11 2024. Zelenskyy especially thanked the Vatican for its humanitarian efforts and Jurash spoke of a „new level of trust in bilateral relations."[22]

---

21 "Messaggio Pasquale del Santo Padre e Benedizione "Urbi et Orbi," March 31, 2024. https://press.vatican.va/content/salastampa/it/bollettino/pubblico/2024/03/31/0265/00555.html#inglese.
22 "Ukrainischer Vatikanbotschafter: Neues Vertrauenslevel." October 13, 2024. https://katholisch.de/artikel/56721-ukrainischer-vatikanbotschafter-neues-vertrauenslevel.

Ukrainian Churches and Religious Communities in the Invasion Overlooked Contributions?

Vladyslav Zaiets

February 2024 marks the 10th anniversary of Russia's aggressive war against Ukraine and the second anniversary of Russia's full-scale, unprovoked, unjustified invasion of Ukraine. The war of aggression, unleashed by the Russian Federation, has brought profound suffering to the Ukrainian land, causing the death of hundreds of thousands of people, the destruction of cities and civil infrastructure, as well as the largest migration crisis in Europe since the Second World War. It has led to the violation of humanitarian law and fundamental rights and freedoms, including freedom of religion, in the temporarily occupied territories of Ukraine.

Churches and religious organizations of Ukraine, being an integral part of Ukrainian society, also became targets of military aggression by the Russian Federation. Dozens of clergymen and representatives of various churches have been killed by the Russian military, and more than 600 religious buildings have been destroyed or damaged due to Russian air, missile and artillery strikes. Clergymen of various denominations, including Greek Catholic priests, ministers of Protestant churches, and representatives of other denominations are being illegally detained in prisons. Preaching in the Ukrainian language is prohibited in the temporarily occupied territories, where a regime of total control over religious activities has been established. Since the beginning of the full-scale invasion, the socially significant activities of churches and religious organizations have become extremely important.

The purpose of this publication is to describe the contribution of various religious communities in Ukraine, including the Ukrainian Greek Catholic Church, the Roman Catholic Church, Protestant churches, Muslim communities, Jewish religious organizations, and Buddhist communities, in repelling Russian aggression against

Ukraine, asserting national identity, and maintaining stability of spirit of the Ukrainian people in their struggle for freedom and independence.

Ukrainian Greek Catholic Church

The Ukrainian Greek Catholic Church (UGCC) is of high importance in the religious life of Ukraine, ranking third in the number of religious organizations behind the Orthodox Church of Ukraine (Metropolitan Epiphany) and the Ukrainian Orthodox Church (Metropolitan Onufriy). The church is part of the Ukrainian Council of Churches and Religious Organizations (UCCRO), whose members include the Roman Catholic Church, other Orthodox and Protestant churches, as well as Jewish and Muslim religious associations.[1]

Since the beginning of the Russian full-scale invasion, the UGCC has played a significant role in supporting the Ukrainian people at the spiritual and humanitarian levels. On the eve of the Russian aggression against Ukraine, the UGCC, along with other denominations in the UCCRO, called on President Vladimir Putin to "stop the raging fire of war"[2]. However, this appeal was ignored by the leadership of the Russian Federation. After that, the Church, both together with other denominations and independently, made statements regarding various aspects of the Russian military aggression against Ukraine and in support of the Ukrainian people. These included an address to Russia's military aggression against Ukraine[3], the Pastoral Message of the Synod of Bishops of the UGCC in Ukraine on patriotism as love for one's people and the

---

[1] See Ukrainian Council of Churches and Religious Organizations. "Information about UCCRO." https://vrciro.org.ua/en/council/info.

[2] Ukrainian Council of Churches and Religious Organizations. "Ukrainian Council of Churches Calls on President Putin to Stop the War." February 23, 2022. https://vrciro.org.ua/en/statements/uccro-calls-on-president-putin-to-stop-the-war.

[3] See Ukrainian Council of Churches and Religious Organizations. "UCCRO Address Regarding Russian Military Aggression Against Ukraine." February 24, 2022. https://vrciro.org.ua/en/statements/uccro-address-regarding-russian-military-aggression-against-ukraine.

Motherland[4], and the Message of the Synod of Bishops of the UGCC in Ukraine regarding war and just peace in the context of new ideologies.[5]

The largest charity structure of the Church, the international charity fund "Caritas Ukraine", provided the needy with food and necessities in the first days of the war, until humanitarian aid from international partners and fellow believers from abroad began to arrive in Ukraine. In addition to Caritas of Ukraine, other charitable structures of the UGCC perform substantial socially significant activities, including the Patriarchal Foundation "Mudra Sprava", "Knights of Columbus", and others.[6]

Considering the latest challenges of wartime and the need for an adequate response to them, the UGCC introduced a mandatory course for clergy, "Healing the Wounds of War", in the fall of 2023. The main goal of the course is to teach priests to provide professional help and care to all those who have suffered because of the war. By the beginning of 2024, 445 clerics of the UGCC in Ukraine had completed the program and received certificates. The "Healing the Wounds of War" program also offers appropriate courses for the wives of priests and monastics of the Church.[7]

The UGCC conducts active advocacy work internationally, both independently and in collaboration with other denominations, spreading accurate information about the war in Ukraine. Efforts include the visit of the UCCRO to the Vatican (January 2023), and meetings of the Conference of European Churches (June 2022) and the USA (November 2023), among others. The Church has developed a system for the pastoral care of Ukrainian refugees in various

---

4   See Synod of Bishops of the UGCC. "Pastoral Message on Patriotism as Love for One's People and the Motherland." December 5, 2022. https://docs.ugcc.ua/1628/.
5   See Synod of Bishops of the UGCC. "Message on War and Just Peace in the Context of New Ideologies." February 16, 2024. https://docs.ugcc.ua/1723/.
6   See Knights of Columbus. "Mercy in Practice—3 Thousand Tons of Aid for Ukraine." April 18, 2023. https://rkc.org.ua/blog/2023/04/18/lyczari-kolumba-i-ukrayina-ponad-rik-solidarnosti-z-postrazhdalymy-vid-vijny/.
7   See Ukrainian Greek Catholic Church. "The Certified Course 'Healing the Wounds of War' for the Clergy of the UGCC Has Started." September 19, 2023. https://ugcc.ua/data/startuvav-sertyfikovanyy-kurs-ztsilennya-ran-viyny-dlya-duhovenstva-ugkts-3582/.

countries due to Russian aggression. Additionally, the UGCC, in cooperation with other Ukrainian churches, religious organizations, and international partners, addresses the issues of post-war reconstruction in Ukraine.

The Roman Catholic Church in Ukraine

The Roman Catholic Church in Ukraine (RCC) has 7 dioceses and over 1,000 religious communities. The RCC actively participates in inter-church dialogue and cooperation through the Ukrainian Council of Churches and Religious Organizations and the Conference of Christian Churches of Ukraine.

Since the beginning of the full-scale invasion, the RCC has condemned Russian aggression against Ukraine. Together with other religious communities in Ukraine,[8] it calls for prayers for a just peace, and spiritually and prayerfully supporting the Ukrainian people in their struggle for freedom and independence.[9]

Through the religious mission "Caritas-Spes" and with the support of international partners, the Church provides humanitarian assistance to broad sections of the population in need and implements charitable projects across various regions of Ukraine. Currently, Caritas Ukraine operates in 23 regions of Ukraine and more than 15,000 settlements, including front-line areas. "Caritas-Spes "[10] is supported by over 100 international partners worldwide. From February 2022 to the present, more than 1.1 million people have received humanitarian aid. In 2023 alone, 950 tons of humanitarian

---

[8] See Roman Catholic Church in Ukraine. "Head of the Conference of Bishops of Ukraine: Any Manifestations of Support for the 'Russian Peace' Are Unacceptable." August 29, 2023. https://rkc.org.ua/blog/2023/08/29/golova-konferen cziyi-yepyskopiv-ukrayiny-bud-yaki-proyavy-pidtrymky-russkogo-myra-nep rypustymi/.

[9] See Roman Catholic Church in Ukraine. "Episcopate of Ukraine: October 27 – We Pray and Fast for Peace." October 21, 2023. https://rkc.org.ua/blog/2023/10/21/ yepyskopat-ukrayiny-27-zhovtnya-molymos-i-postymo-v-namiri-myru/.

[10] The founders of this mission are the Conference of Bishops of the RCC in Ukraine. Therefore, Caritas Ukraine and Caritas-Spes are legally different, but ideologically they form a single system of charitable assistance.

goods were distributed and 360,000 people received charitable aid.[11]

The priests of the RCC provide for the spiritual needs of servicemen and their families as full-time military and volunteer chaplains of the public organization "Christian Salvation Service", which includes clergymen of various churches and is an example of cooperation and mutual understanding between churches in serving the Defense Forces of Ukraine.[12]

Representatives of the RCC participate in the state-church dialogue in Ukraine and in advocacy events at the international level like visits of UCCRO delegations to Berlin and Brussels (2022), to the Vatican (2023) and to the USA (2023).

Protestant churches of Ukraine

Protestant churches in Ukraine are represented by a wide range of denominations: Baptists, Pentecostals, Adventists, Charismatics, Lutherans, Reformers, and others. Protestant religious communities constitute approximately 30% of all religious organizations in Ukraine. The largest associations of Protestant (Evangelical) churches in Ukraine are the All-Ukrainian Union of the Churches of Evangelical Christian-Baptist (AUUCECB), the Ukrainian Pentecostal Church (UPC), and the Ukrainian Union Conference of the Seventh-day Adventist Church (UUCSDAC). Most Protestant churches in Ukraine are affiliated with the Council of Evangelical Protestant Churches of Ukraine. They are actively involved in interfaith dialogue and cooperation, particularly within the Ukrainian Council of Churches and Religious Organizations and the Conference of Christian Churches of Ukraine.

In February 2023, the World Evangelical Alliance, the European Evangelical Alliance, and the Council of Evangelical

---

11 See Caritas-Spes Ukraine. "Results of Emergency Response Projects." https://caritas-spes.org/en/page/war
12 See Roman Catholic Church in Ukraine. "Corps of Peacemakers: Activity of Believers in Wartime." October 1, 2022. https://rkc.org.ua/blog/2022/10/01/korpus-myrotvorcziv-aktyvnist-viryan-u-chasi-vijny/.

Protestant Churches of Ukraine issued a joint statement condemning the Russian invasion of Ukraine. The statement expressed gratitude to those helping the victims and called for the withdrawal of Russian troops from Ukrainian territory, as well as urging prayers for peace and the post-war reconstruction of Ukraine while encouraging Russian Christians to reflect on their actions in light of Christian values. In February 2024, the Council of Evangelical Protestant Churches of Ukraine called to "fight for the complete defeat of the enemy, the restoration of the territorial integrity of Ukraine and the establishment of a just peace", thereby addressing the 10th anniversary of the beginning of the war.[13]

With the support of international partners and using their own resources since the first day of the full-scale Russian invasion, Protestant churches have been providing charitable assistance to the needy and victims of the war. Volunteers from evangelical churches have been actively assisting with the evacuation of people from war zones to safe regions of Ukraine for over two years. In safe locations, displaced refugees are provided with spiritual, psychological, and humanitarian aid, as well as assistance in adaptation and employment in a new environment.

The charity fund "Save Ukraine! " in which representatives of various Protestant churches work on a volunteer basis with the assistance of international partners and with the support of evangelical communities of Ukraine evacuated more than 110,000 people from the war zone, returned 515 children from the Russian Federation to Ukraine, and raised approximately 10 million dollars for humanitarian projects in Ukraine.[14]

Representatives of Protestant churches in Ukraine are actively involved at the international level in conveying accurate information about the war in Ukraine, the Russian Federation's crimes against humanity. Notably, leaders of the evangelical churches of

---

13 See Evangelical Christians-Baptists of Ukraine. "Joint Statement of the CEA, EEA and REPCU on the Anniversary of the Russian Invasion." October 1, 2022. https://www.chve.org.ua/repcu_zayava-24-02-23/.

14 See Save Ukraine. "Charitable Fund 'Save Ukraine!'" https://www.saveukrain eua.org/about-us/.

Ukraine participated in the international religious freedom summits in Washington (USA) in 2023 and 2024,[15] as well as the OSCE Conference on the Human Dimension in Warsaw (Poland) in September 2023, among others.

Muslim communities of Ukraine

The Muslim community of Ukraine is represented by various spiritual (religious) administrations. The most famous are the Spiritual Administration of Muslims of the Autonomous Republic of Crimea (SAMARC) and the Spiritual Administration of Muslims of Ukraine (SAMU), also known as "Umma". SAMU and SAMARC are members of the Ukrainian Council of Churches and Religious Organizations and actively participate in interfaith dialogue and cooperation.

Since the beginning of the full-scale invasion, Muslim spiritual centers have condemned Russia's aggression against Ukraine with collective and individual statements. They have also called for prayers for peace and engaged in advocacy activities at the international level. Sheikh Ahmed Tamim, the Head of the Religious Administration of Ukrainian Muslims, participated in visits to Berlin and Brussels (June 2022) as well as to the USA (November 2023) as part of the UCCRO delegation, among others.[16] In February 2023, the mufti of SAMARC Ayder Rustemov emphasized the problems of forced mobilization of Crimean Tatars by the Russian authorities, resulting in a significant number of people being forced to flee Crimea. He also noted cases of torture of representatives of the Crimean Tatar religious community who have become victims of violence during the Russian occupation of Crimea.[17]

---

15 See Ukrainian Council of Churches and Religious Organizations. "Ukrainian Religious Leaders Spoke in the USA about Russian Repression in the Occupied Territories." October 31, 2023. https://vrciro.org.ua/en/news/2023-uccro-meeting-in-washington.
16 See Ukrainian Council of Churches and Religious Organizations. "The Delegation of the Ukrainian Council of Churches Held Meetings at the White House and USCIRF." November 2, 2023. https://vrciro.org.ua/ua/events/uccro-meetings-at-white-house-and-uscirf.
17 See Gordeev, Oleksiy, "Mufti of the Spiritual Administration of the Muslims of the Autonomous Republic of Crimea Ayder Rustemov: 'The Crimean Tatars

From February 2022 to the present, Muslims in Ukraine have been providing humanitarian aid to war victims, helping them settle into new places of residence, actively engaging in volunteer activities, and providing spiritual support to Muslim servicemen.

Jewish religious communities of Ukraine

Jewish religious communities are represented in Ukraine by several associations that reflect the diversity of Judaism and its various currents. The main Jewish religious associations in Ukraine are the Union of Jewish Religious Organizations of Ukraine (UJROU), the Federation of Jewish Communities of Ukraine, the All-Ukrainian Congress of Jewish Religious Communities, and the Association of Communities of Progressive Judaism of Ukraine. These Jewish communities engage in religious life and are active participants in interfaith dialogue and cooperation in Ukraine.

Since the beginning of the large-scale invasion, the Jewish religious communities of Ukraine have condemned Russian aggression against Ukraine and actively participated in humanitarian projects to support the population.

Chief Rabbi of Ukraine, Moshe Reuven Asman, who also leads the All-Ukrainian Congress of Jewish Religious Communities (Hasidic Chabad Lubavitch), expressed his outrage in a video message, questioning Russia's claim of '*denazify*'. He asked, "*From whom: from local Russians or Jews?*" — pointing out the absurdity of Russia's justification for its invasion. Rabbi Asman shared the personal story of Zorik (Zoreslav Zamoyskyi), a member of Kyiv's Brodsky Synagogue, who was killed in Bucha during the Russian occupation in

---

who remained on the peninsula are our capacity to resist the Russians in the guerrilla war.'" February 16, 2023. https://risu.ua/muftij-duhovnogo-upravlinnya-musulman-avtonomnoyi-respubliki-krim-ajder-rustemov-krimski-tatari-y aki-zalishilisya-na-pivostrovi--ce-nash-potential-oporu-rosiyanam-u-partizanskij-vijni_n136799.

April 2022. He highlighted Zorik as one of the many innocent victims of Russian atrocities in cities like Bucha, Irpin, and Borodyanka.[18]

> "It is obvious to us that Russia strives to destroy Ukrainians in general as a nation, as the people of Ukraine, as well as to destroy any idea of an independent Ukrainian state. After the collapse of the Soviet Union, democracy began to flourish in Ukraine, true freedom of religion appeared, and religious pluralism was established. However, now Russia seeks to destroy all and is establishing the ideology of 'Russian Peace' in the occupied territories of Ukraine, which involves the complete destruction of Ukrainian identity and brutal repression against all those disloyal to the occupiers and all religious minorities",

said Yaakov Dov Bleich, Chief Rabbi of Kyiv and Ukraine UJROU at a panel discussion at the US Institute of Peace in Washington.[19]

In September 2023, President of Ukraine Volodymyr Zelenskyy met with 32 rabbis from various Jewish communities to emphasize the unity of the Jewish community in Ukraine and to underscore the role of the Jewish communities in aiding Ukrainians and in organizing various humanitarian projects.[20]

Summary

During the war, Ukrainian churches and religious organizations act as active and effective institutions of civil society, maintaining a high level of public trust. Amidst the full-scale Russian invasion, religious communities show love for their neighbor in practice, providing spiritual and material help to everyone who needs it. These religious communities, which are part of Ukrainian society

---

18 See Zaiets, Alexander et al. eds. Russian Attack on Religious Freedom in Ukraine: Research, Analysis and Recommendations. Kyiv: O. V. Pugach, 2022. https://irf.in.ua/files/publications/2022.09-IRF-Ukraine-report-UKR.pdf.
19 See Ukrainian Council of Churches and Religious Organizations. "Ukrainian Religious Leaders Spoke in the USA about Russian Repression in the Occupied Territories." October 31, 2023. https://vrciro.org.ua/en/news/2023-uccro-meeting-in-washington.
20 See Ukrainian Jewish Community. "Zelenskyy Met with Representatives of the Ukrainian Jewish Community." November 21, 2024. https://www.ukrinform.ua/rubric-society/3761409-zelenskij-zustrivsa-z-predstavnikami-ukrainskoi-evrejskoi-gromadi.html.

and may be considered unheard or overlooked, are in fact an integral part of the support and recovery efforts, playing a crucial role in helping those affected by the war. Not only do they not go unheard, but they are part of a vital group that helps in times of war, contributing to both the spiritual well-being and physical survival of the Ukrainian people.

Churches and religious organizations have developed collective and individual projects to support the Ukrainian people, certain population groups and individuals during the war. Interfaith dialogue and cooperation between different faiths in Ukraine continues to evolve, setting an example and contributing to the consolidation of Ukrainian society amidst today's challenges.

Among the more than 250 military chaplains in the Armed Forces of Ukraine, many are representatives from the UGCC, RCC, Protestant churches, Jewish and Muslim associations. This allows the needs of all servicemen in the Defence Forces of Ukraine to be met, with volunteer chaplains making a very important contribution to addressing the spiritual needs of servicemen and their families, as exemplified by organizations like the "Christian Rescue Service".

Ukrainian churches, in collaboration with various charitable organizations and authorities, are actively working to facilitate the return of Ukrainian children from the Russian Federation. However, the return of Ukrainian civilians from Russian captivity remains very difficult, requiring the attention and joint action of the international community. Moreover, Ukrainian churches and religious organizations continue to provide spiritual and humanitarian support to the Ukrainian people as they resist Russian aggression. They are also committed to promoting a just peace for Ukraine and are comprehensively preparing for the nation's post-war reconstruction.

Ukrainian Free Churches after the Invasion
The Power of National Reinvention?

Joshua T. Searle and Oleksandr Geychenko

I. Introduction

Ever since the collapse of the Soviet Union, Ukrainians have faced a choice: to align with a democratic Europe or with an autocratic Russia. Since the first Russian invasion of Ukraine in 2014, the Free Churches of Ukraine have spearheaded a movement aimed at freeing Ukrainian society from the burdensome legacy of Soviet totalitarianism and steering it towards full integration into the European democratic family of nations. Since the beginning of Russia's illegal full-scale war of aggression in 2022, this trend has gained new urgency and impetus, with Free Church thinking assuming significant public relevance.

This chapter aims to highlight the increased social prominence and significance of the free churches in Ukraine since the invasion in February 2022. We argue that, despite their relatively small numbers,[1] Ukrainian Free Church Christians have played a pivotal role in helping Ukraine forge a new national and European identity, distinct from its Russian and Soviet past.[2]

To understand how and why Free Church thinking has become more prominent in the public sphere, it is necessary first to

---

[1] According to the statistics provided by two larger unions — All-Ukrainian Union of Churches of Evangelical Christians-Baptists and Ukrainian Church of Christians of Evangelical Faith (Pentecostals) — they comprised of 3,907 churches (2,177 and 1730 respectively) and 205,648 members (104,042 and 101,606 respectively). This data does not include churches on the occupied territories and in Crimea.

[2] In this chapter, we use the term "Free Churches" to refer to Protestant Christian denominations and congregations in Ukraine and Russia that are not affiliated with a specific state or government authority. They seek to operate independently from state interference or control in matters of church governance, beliefs and worship practices. Some examples of Free Churches that are notable in the context of Russia and Ukraine include Baptists, Methodists, Congregationalists, and Pentecostals.

offer some summary remarks concerning how Christians from the Free Churches have historically viewed their duties and responsibilities towards the state and society. Accordingly, after a brief historical overview of the origins and development of the Free Church movement in Russia and Ukraine, the first part of this chapter addresses the question of how Free Churches approach questions of power, paying particular attention to the categorical rejection of coercion in matters of faith and public witness. The chapter continues with an analysis of how these Free Church convictions have found new resonance in Ukrainian society due to the existential threat posed by Russia and the Russian Orthodox Church. We contend that underlying the Russo-Ukrainian War is a deep-seated clash of two antithetical visions of Christianity: state-endorsed Christendom versus Open Christianity.[3] The chapter then provides a brief historical overview of the Free Churches in Ukraine and Russia, attempting to account for the differences in perspectives on questions of power, authority and relations to the state. We conclude with a theological assessment of how the war has expanded the understanding of mission and evangelism among the Ukrainian free churches.

II. Historical Context of Free Churches in Ukraine and Russia

A. Overview of the History of Free Churches in Ukraine and Russia

The evangelical movement emerged independently in three regions of the Russian Empire—Ukraine, Trans-Caucasia, and St. Petersburg—in the late 19th century.[4] The number of Free Church Christians in the Russian Empire increased steadily during this period,

---

[3] On the concept of "Open Church" see Moltmann, Jürgen. *The Open Church: Invitation to a Messianic Life-Style*. London, 1978 and Wright, Nigel G. *New Baptists, New Agenda*. Carlisle, 2002, 64-80.

[4] See Coleman, Heather J. "Baptist Beginnings in Russia and Ukraine." *Baptist History and Heritage* 42, no. 1 (2007): 24–36, 24. The Orthodox priests report by 1884 2,000 Baptists in Kyiv and 3,000 in Kherson gubernia, who by 1891 grew by 5,000, Klibanov, A. I. *Istoriiā religioznogo sektantstva v Rossii*. Moscow, 1965, 208. The area expanded: in 1884 Baptists were in 95 villages in Kherson gubernia and by 1891 spread to 167 villages. By 1890s Baptists were present in 30

reaching approximately 20,000 Baptists among the Russian population by 1905. Following the Edict of Toleration (1905), the Free Churches prospered, spreading their faith and communities across the Russian Empire. The years from 1917 to 1928, termed the "Golden Age", saw significant growth, particularly among Baptists.[5] However, after 1928, the Free Churches faced severe repression under Stalin.[6] The government's interference stifled organisational structures, and the crackdown on evangelism in the 1920s and 30s led to the persecution and closure of churches, culminating in the near eradication of organised religious activities by 1939.[7]

Following the Second World War, the Soviet authorities sought to tighten control over religious activities. From the late

---

gubernias of the Russian Empire, Klibanov, 1965, 207. In 1905 at the first World Baptist Congress in London Dei Mazaev reported 20,000 Baptists among Russians, see Mitrokhin, L. N. *Baptizm: istoriiā i sovremennost'. Filosofsko-sotsiologicheskie ocherki.* St. Petersburg, 1997, 250.

5 See Steeves, Paul D. *The Russian Baptist Union, 1917–1935: Evangelical Awakening in Russia.* Kansas, 1977, 99–100; see also Prokhorov, Konstantin. "The 'Golden Age' of the Soviet Baptists in the 1920s." In *Eastern European Baptist History: New Perspectives*, edited by Sharyl Corrado, Praha, 2007, 88–101. According to Prokhorov quantitative growth during "Golden Age" was an indirect result of the Bolsheviks' efforts to demolish Russian Orthodox Church.

6 See Mitrokhin, L. N. Mitrokhin, L. N. *Baptizm: istoriiā i sovremennost'. Filosofsko-sotsiologicheskie ocherki.* St. Petersburg, 1997, 389–391. It should be noted that restrictions began in the early 1920s when Soviet officials began requesting mandatory registration of religious communities. In 1923 the government made Baptist and Evangelical Christians change position on military service, see *TSerkov' dolzhna ostavat'siā tserkov'iū: neobratimye desiātiletiiā 1917–1937 gg. v istorii evangel'skogo i baptistskogo dvizhenii. Istoriko-analiticheskiĭ otdel MSTS EKhB*, 2008, 36–49; Coleman, Heather J. *The Most Dangerous Sect: Baptists in Tsarist and Soviet Russia, 1905–1929.* Illinois, 1998, 295–297. In 1924 Bolsheviks formed the League of the Militant Godless (LMG) to win the public through mass atheistic propaganda. More on the LMG see in Pospielovsky, Dimitry V. *A History of Marxist-Leninist Atheism and Soviet Antireligious Policies. A History of Soviet Atheism in Theory and Practice and the Believer.* Vol. 1. Basingstoke, London, 1987, 49–68. For Ukrainian context see Panchenko, V., and Roman A. Sitarchuk. 'Deiāki aspekty derzhavno-tserkovnykh vidnosyn u 20-30-ti rr. KhKh st. (na prykladi hromad baptystiv ta iēvanhel's'kyĭ khrystyiān Poltavshchyny)'. *Z arkhiviv VUChK-HPU-KHB* 20 (2003): 278–86.; Holoshchapova, IĒ. O. 'Hromady iēvanhel's'kykh khrystyiān-baptystiv v umovakh suspil'nykh transformatsiĭ 20-30kh rr. XX st.' Avtoreferat dysertatsiĭ, Zaporiz'kyĭ natsional'nyĭ universytet, 2010.

7 See Kolarz, Walter. *Religion in the Soviet Union.* London, 1961.

1940s to the mid-1980s, Free Churches, including Protestant denominations like Baptists and Pentecostals, faced severe persecution and restrictions.[8] The Soviet authorities viewed these religious groups with suspicion, considering them threats to the state ideology. Places of worship were often surveilled and closed down. Religious leaders were arrested, imprisoned, or forced into exile. The period saw a systematic campaign to suppress religious freedom and eradicate religious influences, leading to a challenging and oppressive environment for Free Churches and pushing them into private spaces and exclusively religious activities. That continued until the *Perestroika* era in the 1980s.

After *Perestroika*, the Free Churches in Russia experienced a period of growth and revival. With increased religious freedom and the loosening of restrictions, these churches saw a surge in membership, church planting, and evangelistic activities. However, this newfound freedom faced challenges during Putin's presidency, as the Russian government began to tighten control over religious institutions and activities.[9] By differentiating between "traditional" and "non-traditional" religions, the Russian government created an instrument of control and manipulation that further restricted religious freedom and activities.

Under the autocracy of Vladimir Putin, the Russian Orthodox Church has dedicated significant efforts to suppress other religious groups by discouraging religious diversity and benefiting from state-endorsed privileges.[10] Despite this monopolisation of religious space and the lingering post-Soviet legacy of suspicion towards Free Church Christians, Russian Protestants in the early 2000s were relatively successful in establishing themselves within their local communities. They enhanced their public visibility and esteem through committed participation in charitable ministries,

---

8   For a reliable and comprehensive account of Soviet persecution of the churches, see Ramet, Sabrina Petra. *Religious Policy in the Soviet Union*. Cambridge, 2005.
9   See Burgess, John P. *Holy Rus': The Rebirth of Orthodoxy in the New Russia*. New Haven, 2017.
10 See Garrard, John, / Garrard, Carol. *Russian Orthodoxy Resurgent: Faith and Power in the New Russia*. Princeton, 2014.

such as operating drug and alcohol rehabilitation centers throughout Russia.¹¹

Following the Russian invasion of Ukraine in 2014, the position of the Russian Free Churches became more problematic, as leaders felt pressured to demonstrate their loyalty and conformity to the Putinist agenda. For instance, after the invasion and annexation of the Ukrainian sovereign territory of Crimea in 2014, the Russian Baptist Union made a statement in support of Putin, expressing their "special gratitude for the fact that the protection and strengthening of spiritual and moral values, which includes the traditional family, [is] identified by you [Putin] as one of the priorities."[12] Even after the full-scale invasion of Ukraine in 2022, the general tendency of the Free Churches in Russia has been to support the Putin regime and to profess loyalty to the Russian state,[13] even praising the Russian dictator as a defender of Christian values.[14] Needless to say, such attitudes have darkened relations between the Russian and Ukrainian Free Churches.[15]

---

11 See Roman Lunkin notes that in 2018, there were around 500 such centres, founded by Protestants, located throughout the Russian Federation. By comparison, the Russian Orthodox Church ran only 70 rehabilitation centres. See Lunkin, Roman. "Why Does the Orthodox Church Fight Against Society in Russia?" *East-West Church Report*, May 5, 2018. https://missioneurasia.ca/articles/roman-lunkin-why-does-the-orthodox-church-fight-against-society-in-russia/. According to Lunkin, Russian Protestants in the early 2000s had become "the most successful in social work and are entrenched in most regions of Russia as one of the leading forces of society." See Lunkin, Roman. "A Reaction of Russian Churches on Ukrainian Crisis: A Prophecy of Democracy." In *Religion, State, Society, and Identity in Transition: Ukraine*, edited by Rob van der Laarse et al., Oisterwijk, 2015, 435–475, 436.

12 Russian Union of Evangelical Christian-Baptists. "Obrashchenie k Prezidentu Rossiĭskoĭ Federatsii V.V. Putinu." June 14, 2014. http://baptist.org.ru/news/main/view/obraschenie-k-prezidentu-rossii-34-sezd.

13 See CNE-News. "Russian Protestants Will Not Condemn War." June 4, 2022. https://cne.news/article/1258-russian-protestants-will-not-condemn-war.

14 See Ryakhovsky, Sergei. " RIA Novosti: V ROSKhVE prokommentirovali poslanie prezidenta Fe-deral'nomu sobraniiū." March 1, 2024. https://www.cef.ru/infoblock/media-digest/newsitem/article/1763033.

15 Attempts to start a dialogue between Russian and Ukrainian believers demonstrated absolutely different perspectives on church-state relations between the sides. See e.g. responses to the special Ukraine theme issue of *East-West Church and Ministry Report*: Canon Michael Bourdeaux et al., eds. *East-West Church & Ministry Report*. Summer 2014. Vol. 22, no. 3. https://www.eastwestreport.org/pdfs/ew22-3.pdf; *East-West Church & Ministry Report*. Fall 2014. Vol.

By contrast, after achieving independence in 1991, Ukraine embraced a more diverse approach and, on an official level, showed greater acceptance toward minority religious communities.[16] However, for the first 25 years after the collapse of the USSR, to be "Christian" for many Ukrainians often meant to be "Orthodox". Like their Russian counterparts, Ukrainian Free Church Christians generally avoided involvement in politics and public engagement, focusing instead on personal spirituality and church-based evangelistic and charitable activities. However, following the Orange Revolution in 2004 and the Revolution of Dignity on Maidan in 2014, the Free Churches in Ukraine, especially Baptists and Pentecostals, became much more engaged in the national life of Ukraine and gained more prominence in the public eye.[17]

This trend of increased visibility and recognition has intensified since the full-scale illegal Russian invasion in February 2022. The newfound esteem and recognition given to Free Churches in Ukraine result from their principled solidarity with Ukrainian society and their laudable commitment to democratic ideals such as civil liberty, free speech, universal human rights, tolerance, and the rule of law.

B.   *The theological-ecclesiological distinctives of free churches*

A fundamental conviction of Free Church faith communities, such as Baptists, is that faith cannot be coerced. Free Church ecclesiology

---

22, no. 4. https://www.eastwestreport.org/pdfs/ew22-4.pdf; *East-West Church & Ministry Report.* Winter 2015. Vol. 23, no. 1. https://www.eastwestreport.org/pdfs/ew23-1.pdf; East-West Church & Ministry Report. Spring 2015. Vol. 23, no. 2. https://www.eastwestreport.org/pdfs/ew23-2.pdf; Canon Michael Bourdeaux et al., eds. *East-West Church Report & Ministery Report.* Summer 2015. Vol. 23, no. 3. https://www.eastwestreport.org/pdfs/ew23-3.pdf.4.

16   See Wanner, Catherine. *Communities of the Converted: Ukrainians and Global Evangelism.* Ithaca, 2011. As recently as March 2024, Ryakhovsky commended Putin's speech to the Federal Assembly, saying that "having listened to the President's message ... I am ready to support such a candidate for President of Russia ... As Evangelical Christians, we will continue to support and implement traditional spiritual and moral values."

17   For an ethnographic description of the diverse ways in which Free Churches have become more visible in Ukrainian society since Maidan, see Wanner, Catherine. *Everyday Religiosity and the Politics of Belonging in Ukraine.* Ithaca, 2022.

maintains that whenever Christian faith is enforced by a church or government, it becomes formal and loses its salvific character. For Free Church Christians, the principles of freedom and dignity are incompatible with the political principles of coercion and domination, even if these principles are framed within a Christian context. They believe that Christ's command to preach the gospel and build the Kingdom of God should be implemented out of love and service, rather than through force, domination, or the endorsement of political power structures.[18]

In both religion and politics, Free Church Christians maintain that any form of Christianity devoid of freedom and dignity is necessarily emptied of its Christian content and assumes dehumanising and unjust forms of domination and control. The theological conviction underlying this commitment is the belief that God has revealed himself to the world in Christ not through power and authority, but through freedom and self-sacrificial love. In the Free Church understanding, people become Christians not through accidents of geography or by state-imposed edicts, but through a free and conscious response of obedience to the Way of Jesus.[19]

III. The Responses of the Free Churches to the Russo-Ukrainian War

A. *The Russian War of Aggression as a Clash of Two Competing Visions of Christianity*

The Free Church convictions summarised above may seem abstract and detached. However, considering the Russian invasion of Ukraine these fundamental beliefs have acquired a new significance. In many ways, the Russo-Ukrainian war represents a civilisational conflict in which two competing ideas of Christianity contend for dominance: (1) the authoritarian-theocratic idea; and (2)

---

18 See Searle, Joshua T. "Baptist Perspectives on Freedom and the Kingdom of God." In *Baptists and the Kingdom of God: World Perspectives Through Four Interpretive Lenses,* edited by T. Laine Scales and João B. Chaves, Waco, TX, 2023, 271–90.

19 See Shurden, Walter B. *The Baptist Identity: Four Fragile Freedoms.* Macon, GA, 1993, 59.

the pluralist-democratic idea. In the first vision, the church and state work in tandem to impose "traditional Christian values" through legislation or even military force. According to this idea of Christianity, the masses are expected to show unquestioning loyalty to autocratic political and ecclesiastical authority. This authoritarian-theocratic vision is based on the ideas of a "state Church" and a "Christian nation" or, in the lexicon of Russian Orthodoxy, "a God-bearing people."[20] The assumption guiding much of Kremlin policy is that by conquering and subduing Ukrainian territory, the Russian state, in collusion with the Russian Orthodox Church, will be able to impose its religious values and political ideology on the occupied populations.

The second version of Christianity, represented by the Free Churches, is based on the idea of freedom. According to this perspective, the notions of a "state Church" or a "Christian nation" are regarded not as sacred archetypes, but as profane illusions. Being principally open to all people, it values spiritual dignity and the inherent worth of all people, regardless of their social status or religious affiliation. Rather than demanding conformity and respect based on its institutional status and political power, this pluralist-democratic vision of Christianity emphasises the need for tolerance and freedom of conscience.[21]

This second vision of Christianity seeks to promote the values of human dignity and human rights, cultural diversity, democracy, justice, fairness, equality, and the rule of law—not only as social virtues but as gospel imperatives. Christians who adhere to this Free Church vision understand the need to demonstrate the benefits of their faith and to defend their position through respectful debate, rather than from a position of power and privilege.[22] From a Free Church perspective, the first vision, despite its appeals to the outward forms of Christian religion, is associated with the spirit of

---

20 Jane Ellis, Jane. *The Russian Orthodox Church: Triumphalism and Defensiveness.* London, 2016, 106.
21 See Garrett, James Leo. *Baptist Theology: A Four-Century Study.* Macon, GA, 2009, 427.
22 See Searle, Joshua T. *Theology After Christendom: Forming Prophets for a Post-Christian Age.* Eugene, OR, 2018, 174.

idolatry. The second, despite its outward affinities with modern secularism and pluralism, is regarded by the Free Churches as more faithful to the Gospel of Christ.[23] Therefore, we contend that beyond the manifest issues of language, culture and geopolitics, the Russo-Ukrainian war can be interpreted at a deeper level as a clash of these antithetical tendencies within Christianity.

B. *Contrasting approaches and convictions of Free Churches in Ukraine and Russia*

The Kremlin's war is fully endorsed by the Russian Orthodox Church, a stance rooted in its typically "symphonic" relations with the State, dating back to the Byzantine Empire.[24] What is harder to explain is the fact that, overall, Russian protestants have endorsed the authoritarian regime of Vladimir Putin despite its anti-Western propaganda, legal nihilism, widespread nationalism and anti-democratic ferment. In a closed society like Russia, where people are afraid to speak out against the government, Christians tend not to talk about social responsibility, justice, truth, freedom, solidarity, or societal transformation. Instead, they turn to discussions about distant and abstract concepts, such as the soul and eternity, which the ruling authorities regard as less threatening topics.[25] Even when Russian Free Church Christians have private misgivings about the "Special Military Operation", the custom is to remain silent, to make any compromises that are necessary to safeguard one's own interests and the wider interests of one's church or denomination by not expressing any dissent.

---

23 See Searle, Joshua T. "A Theological Case for Ukraine's European Integration: Deconstructing the Myth of 'Holy Russia' vs. 'Decadent Europe.'" *International Journal of Public Theology* 16, no. 3 (2022): 289–304.
24 See e.g. excellent analysis of Orthodox political theology by Papanikolaou, Aristotle. *The Mystical as Political: Democracy and Non-Radical Orthodoxy.* Notre Dame, IN, 2012, 13-54; and by Hovorun, Cyril. *Political Orthodoxies: The Unorthodoxies of the Church Coerced.* Minneapolis, MN, 2018, 66-87.
25 See Searle, Joshua T. / Mykhailo N. Cherenkov. *A Future and a Hope: Mission, Theological Education and the Transformation of Post-Soviet Society.* Eugene, OR, 2014, 67.

The Free Churches in Ukraine, largely due to the Russian invasion, have followed a very different path. Thanks to the endeavours of an "influential minority"[26] of Free Church theologians and church leaders, the idea of an Open Church that serves as a pillar of freedom and democracy, rather than as a closed institution that protects the parochial interests of a corrupt Church-State establishment, has become embedded into the cultural awareness of the Ukrainian people. Within Ukraine, this essentially Free Church perspective is gaining traction among Christians beyond the Free Church tradition. Leading Ukrainian Catholic and Orthodox theologians have advocated from within their own traditions for a vision of the church in society that abandons the Christendom-laden assumptions of the past.[27]

The response of the Ukrainian Free Churches to Russia's ongoing war of aggression against Ukraine since 2014 signals a seismic shift in the public engagement of the churches in post-Soviet society. A movement that began at Maidan in 2013-14 has culminated in a new situation in which the Free Churches of Ukraine

---

26 The idea of Free Church Christians as an "influential minority" within Ukrainian society was introduced by the forward-thinking Ukrainian theologian, Mykhailo Cherenkov as early as 2009: Mikhail, Cherenkov. Kul'tura vliiãtel'nogo men'shinstva. Simferopol': Assotsiatsiia "Dukhovnoe vozrozhdenie", 2010. I (Searle) have described some of the shifting trends in Ukrainian missiology in more detail in my article, "Freedom, Compassion, and Creativity: New Points of Departure for Public Theology in the Post-Soviet Space." *International Journal of Public Theology* 14 (2020): 255–275.

27 See, for example, "A Declaration on the 'Russian World' (Russkii mir) Teaching." March 13, 2022. https://publicorthodoxy.org/2022/03/13/a-declaration-on-the-russian-world-russkii-mir-teaching/. See also "A Statement of Solidarity with the Orthodox Declaration on the 'Russian World' (Russkii Mir) Teaching, and against Christian Nationalism and New Totalitarianism." April 6, 2022. https://publicorthodoxy.org/2022/04/06/russkii-mir-solidarity-statement/; see two appeals of the representatives of evangelical theological educational institutions: Geychenko, Oleksandr et al. "Voices from the Ruins: Appeal of the Representatives of Ukrainian Evangelical Theological Educational Institutions Regarding the War of the Russian Federation against Ukraine." 2022. https://eeit-edu.info/en/appeal-2022/; and Dyaltik, Helga, et al. "Breaking Through the Sound of Air Raid Sirens: Appeal of the Representatives of Ukrainian Evangelical Theological Educational Institutions to the World Evangelical Community Regarding the War of the Russian Federation against Ukraine." November 2022. https://eeit-edu.info/en/appeal-2022-breaking-through-the-sound-of-air-raid-sirens/.

have largely abandoned the Soviet legacy that had assigned evangelical Christians a marginal status as a "sect" or as a foreign presence in post-Soviet society.[28] The Russian invasion, despite its devastating consequences, has served as a powerful impetus for the Free Churches to engage in the public life of the Ukrainian nation.[29] As the Free Churches have rediscovered their prophetic voice, they have recognized that a serious commitment to mission means not only entreating individuals to repent, but also expressing solidarity with the Ukrainian people in their just struggle for dignity and freedom.[30]

IV. Conclusion: How the War has Expanded the Scope of Mission in the thinking of the Ukrainian Free Churches

The Russian war of aggression has facilitated an expansion of the scope of mission in the thinking of the Ukrainian Free Churches. Once considered practically synonymous with "evangelization," the term "mission" within post-Maidan Ukraine now encompasses the role of the church as a prophetic voice in public debate. Thanks to the contributions of an emerging generation of Ukrainian Free

---

28 See "Declaration of Dissent", cited in Cherenkov, Mykhailo. "Protestantism and Protest: Socio-Theological Re-Identification of Ukraine and Ukrainian Protestantism in the Context of Maidan." In *Religion, State, Society, and Identity in Transition – Ukraine*, edited by Rob van der Laarse et al., Oisterwijk, 2015, 319–341, 323f.

29 See, for example, the "Declaration of Dissent", published by a group of Ukrainian Free Church theologians during the Maidan Uprising in December 2013 gave lucid expression to the new thinking within the evangelical movement in Ukraine: "The Baptist Church, from the very first days of its existence, has stood up for freedom and justice. The independence of the Church from the state [...] does not mean political indifference, asociality, or isolation of the Church from the society. Ukrainian Baptists welcomed the independence of Ukraine and have served our nation through the social and spiritual potential of church communities [...] Christians cannot be apart or 'neutral', when authorities abuse their own power, when peaceful people's blood is shed, when courts make unconstitutional decisions, when security forces defend not the people, but the authorities. Participation in demonstrations is the personal responsibility of each believer; this responsibility is inseparable from faith, and expresses itself in civil liability."

30 See Cherenkov, 2015, 340.

Church theologians, there is a new awareness of the necessary connection between Christian mission and the economic, cultural, social and political conditions in the life of the nation as a whole.[31] The challenge for the Ukrainian Free Churches in the years ahead is to respond to the threat from Russia by strengthening Ukraine's connection to the Christian ideals of European civilization, thereby facilitating Ukraine's full integration into the European family of democratic nations.

The Ukrainian Free Churches are linked to the global evangelical movement, which offers a compelling alternative to the parochialism of Russian and post-Soviet Christianity with its burdensome legacy of corruption and compromise. Moreover, the global evangelical community—of which the Free Churches are an integral part—can offer Ukrainians a wealth of experience of holistic missiology and inspiring stories of how the gospel has shaped the destinies of nations. The hope underlying this chapter is that Ukraine's own experience may become one of those stories, serving as an inspiration for Russian Free Church Christians to finally renounce their allegiance to Soviet and Putinist authoritarianism. The responsibility for this possibility lies with those Christians in both nations who recognise that the cause of the gospel is best served not by a "Special Military Operation", but by living in an open society and standing up for the dignity and freedom of all people.

---

[31] Notable examples include Dimid, Mihajlo. Bogoslov'â Svobodi. Ukraïns'ka Versiâ. L'viv, 2020 and Denisenko, Anatoliĭ. Teologiiā Vizvolenniā: Ideï, Kritika, Perspektivi. Kyiv: Dukh i Litera, 2019., as well as the numerous contributions of Mykhailo Cherenkov, such as his book, TSelostnaiā missiiā v usloviiākh voĭny. Irpin, 2017. See also the proceedings of two conferences on the issue of theology of citizenship in Ivano-Frankivsk (September 16-17, 2022) and Bucha (December 20 2023): Materialy mizhnarodnoï naukovo-praktychnoï konferentsiï, TSerkva na shliākhu do formuvanniā bohoslov'iā natsiï ta hromadiānstva. (Ivano-Frankivs'k: Millennium, 2023); Identychnist', etnos, natsiiā. Spetsvypusk, Bohomysliiē 34 (2024): 1.

Islam and Muslims in the Russian War of Aggression
Jihad Against Ukraine?

Andreas Jacobs

1. Introduction

Politics and propaganda in relation to Islam are often overlooked components of Russian efforts to instrumentalize religion in the war of aggression against Ukraine. However, the strengthening and revaluation of Christian Orthodox identity accompanying the war and the increasing involvement of the Russian Orthodox Church (ROC) in the ideological, historical, and religious justification of the war left no room for addressing and involving the estimated 15 to 20 million people in Russia who feel that they belong to Islam. In fact, Islam and Muslims play a significant role in the war against Ukraine, both within Russia and in Russian foreign policy. The horrific Islamist terrorist attacks of March 2024 near Moscow have not changed this situation in any way. Based on a historical classification, the following text outlines the essential elements of Russian religious policy towards Muslims (hereafter referred to as "Islam policy") and illustrates the specific functions of this policy.

2. From Islam in Russia to Russian Islam

2.1 History of Islam in Russia

There is evidence of the presence of Muslims on the territory of present-day Russia as early as the 7th century – two centuries before Christianity. The majority of Russian Muslims belong to indigenous ethnic groups, but their Islamization did not take place until the Middle Ages. The settlement areas of these ethnic groups largely came under Russian control between the 15th and 18th centuries. These areas initially included the Volga region, the Urals and western Siberia, and later Crimea, parts of Ukraine and the Caucasus. At the end of the 18th century, the tsarist empire took these incorporations into account in terms of religious policy. With the "Orenburg Muslim Spiritual Assembly" (OMSA), Russia's links to Islamic culture were made official by Catherine the Great in 1788 and corresponding institutions were founded.[1] However, this did not lead to long-term peace, especially in the North Caucasus. Accordingly, it was generally the Muslim ethnic groups living there who were the victims of tsarist and Stalinist expulsions and persecution and whose problematic relationship with the Russian central state in the Chechen wars of the 1990s and, via the special role of the president of the Chechen republic, Ramzan Kadyrov, in the current war against Ukraine, continues to have an impact to this day.

2.1 Organization of Islam in Russia

The establishment of state-recognized or controlled institutions of Islamic religious practice that took place with the OMSA was expressed above all in the so-called "Islamic administrations" (muftiates), which still play a central role in Russian Islam policy. Each Muslim-majority republic maintains such a muftiate under the leadership of a legal scholar (mufti), whereby some of these muftiates have been in competition with each other since Soviet times due to unclear regional responsibilities and inconsistent access to state resources, or they are organized in partially competing umbrella organizations. The state actively promotes this competition through privileges, financial aid, and political gestures as instruments of loyalty politics. Scholars from the late Soviet and KGB-controlled network of the muftiate in Ufa, which is still controlled by the Kremlin presidential administration, play a special role here.[2] With the help of this network the Kremlin was able to push forward with the political objective of a "Russian Islam" — that is the

---

1 See Laruelle, Marlène. "Russia's Islam: Balancing Securitization and Integration." Russie.Nei.Visions, No. 125. Ifri, Paris, 2021, 8.
2 See Kemper, Michael. "Islam in Russland." Bundeszentrale für politische Bildung, June 14, 2023. https://www.bpb.de.

goal of pushing back the influence of foreign Islamic actors in Russia—through financial donations, state-initiated mosque construction projects, the establishment of state-controlled Islamic schools and universities, from the 2000s onwards.[3]

3. Russian Islam policy under Putin

3.1 The fight against Islamism

The efforts over the past two decades to ensure close state control and conformity of the muftiates and to establish an Islam that is loyal to the Russian state must be seen against the backdrop of the wars in the North Caucasus in the 1990s. In particular, the Islamist terrorism that emerged against the backdrop of the Chechen wars in several bloody attacks in Russia (such as those in Budyonnovsk in 1995, Moscow in 2002, and Beslan in 2004) led to a reorientation of Russian Islam policy at the time. Above all, the attacks on Moscow apartment buildings blamed on Chechen terrorists provided the new President of the Russian Federation, Vladimir Putin, with a welcome opportunity in 1999 to present himself as a tough "savior of Russia".[4]

As a result of this reorientation, Islamist fighters, dissident preachers and foreign donors were increasingly pushed back or silenced. A core of Islamist fighters from the post-Soviet region left for other countries in the Middle East at the end of the 2010s, particularly during the upheavals of the "Arab Spring" and joined the so-called "Islamic State" (IS) in Syria and Iraq. The most prominent example of this migration movement was the Georgian-born Chechen and ex-military man Tarchan Batirashvili, who became one of the best-known leaders of the Islamic State as Abu Omar al-Shishani. After al-Shishani was killed in US airstrikes in the summer of 2016, a former commander-in-chief of the Russian special police replaced him as IS's "Minister of War".

The prominent role of Islamists from the post-Soviet region in IS's war is no coincidence. Militarily trained, battle-hardened, and

---

3 See Kemper 2023.
4 Ibid.

often radicalized in Russian prisons, they had completely different practical and mental capabilities than the often young and militarily inexperienced "foreign fighters" from Western countries. The occurrence of fighters from the post-Soviet region, therefore, also plays a certain role in explaining the Russian intervention in the Syrian civil war on the side of Bashar al-Assad. After all, this was an opportunity to take military action against potential returnees outside their own territory.

3.2 Russian Islam

An important element in the fight against Islamism under Putin was the extensive "nationalization" of Islamic institutions and discourse in Russia. Putin himself repeatedly emphasized Islam as an integral ("traditional") part of Russian culture and history, thus distinguishing it from a "foreign" and "radical" Islam.[5] Analogous to the "Russki Mir" ideology, a narrative was thus established that classified Islam as a constitutive element of a Eurasian space. While Islamic institutions and actors who resisted this nationalization were largely eliminated, state institutions and the state-affiliated muftiates drove forward the construction of this "Russian Islam" (russkii Islam).[6] Based on older efforts to construct a Soviet-compatible interpretation of Islam, Islamic education, financing, organization and even theology were placed under state control from the 2000s onwards.[7]

The main elements of "Russian Islam" were militant patriotism mixed with Islamic symbolism and anti-Western rhetoric. In particular, the rejection of ostensibly "Western" values and behavior became a central bridging narrative in this construction. The common

---

5   See Laruelle 2021, 5 and Sibgatullina, Gulnaz. "The Muftis and the Myths: Constructing the Russian 'Church for Islam'." Problems of Post-Communism, March 22, 2023. https://doi.org/10.1080/10758216.2023.2185899, 1.
6   Regarding the analogy between "Russki Mir" and "Russkii Islam" ideology see Geraev, Danis. "The Methodology of the 'Russian World' and 'Russian Islam': New Ideologies of the Post-Socialist Context." The Soviet and the Post-Soviet Review 48 (2021): 367–90.
7   See Laruelle 2021, 24.

opposition to liberal ideas and modern human rights also consolidated the cooperation between Russian state Islam and the ROC. In many cases, this cooperation went beyond an alliance of convenience and resulted in efforts to establish a church-like Islamic institution analogous to the ROC[8], which stood alongside the state as a religious-political junior partner. Observers describe this as an attempt to establish an "ecumenical partnership".[9] In the "conservative turn" promoted by Putin, many Russian Muslims thus became important allies in the culture war. This explains the high approval ratings for Putin in the Muslim regions of Russia[10] as well as the reaction of the Russian leadership to the Islamist attack on March 22, 2024, in which at least 145 people were killed. On the one side, Russian government propaganda tried to establish a narrative of Ukrainian and Western involvement in the attacks. On the other side, Russian officials emphasized the fact that this form of terrorism affects many Muslim countries as well.

3.3 Kadyrovism

Chechen President Ramzan Kadyrov has played a central role in the Russian fight against Islamism at home and abroad for twenty years. With the help of a habitual and rhetorical appropriation of Islam, Kadyrov established a specific form of interpretation of Islam and loyalty to Putin, which is referred to as "Kadyrovism" in academic debates[11]. The central element of the dual strategy of Islamization and "loyalization" is the personal relationship between Kadyrov and Putin. This relationship is based less on sympathy or ideology than on a congruence of power-political interests. For Putin, Kadyrov is the ideal figure to control the Muslim and ethnic groups in the Caucasus region on the one hand and to construct the fiction of an "Islam-friendly" Russia at home and abroad on the other. For Kadyrov, the alliance with Putin means a considerable increase in power in the internal Chechen power struggle. This

---

8   See Sibgatullina 2023, 2 and 5.
9   Laruelle 2021, 24.
10 See Laruelle 2021, 19.
11 See Laruelle 2021, 21.

power increased further with the Russian invasion of Ukraine. Kadyrov used the initial phase of the war, which was disappointing from a Russian perspective, to build up his battle-hardened private army into an important factor in Putin's takeover plans for Ukraine.[12] Simultaneously, he became an important figure in Russian war propaganda by securing the religious justification for the war of aggression by classifying it as a "holy war" and as the "duty of all Muslims".[13]

However, it is not so much his religious appearance that seems to have an effect here, but rather his machismo-like self-presentation, which creates a bridge between supposedly Russian and Muslim ideas of masculinity. Kadyrov's role in the Ukraine conflict also highlights the limitations and challenges of the Putin regime's close alliance with the Chechen leader. His presumption of religious scholarship and his open contempt for those Chechens and Muslims who are not fighting on Russia's side against Ukraine are increasingly met with disapproval by some religious scholars and his internal Chechen rivals. According to observers, this could reignite the barely suppressed internal Chechen conflicts in the medium term.[14]

3.4 Russian-Middle Eastern alliances

Kadyrov also plays an important role in the international campaign for support for the Russian war of aggression. He maintains good contacts with Saudi Arabia in particular and promotes himself there as a "servant of the holy Quran".[15] With this self-portrayal, he has been able to achieve significant successes and provide religious rhetorical cover for Russia's attempts at rapprochement with the

---

[12] See Heß, Miriam Katharina. "Wie Russland den Islam und innerstaatliche Konflikte instrumentalisiert: Strategien in Russlands Krieg gegen die Ukraine und ihre Folgen." DGAP Policy Brief No. 13, May 4, 2023, 2 and Laruelle, Marlène. "Russia at War and the Islamic World." Russie.Nei.Visions, No. 127. Ifri, Paris, 2023, 8.
[13] See Gaspar, Hande Abay, and Manjana Sold. "Der Ukraine-Krieg in der islamistischen Propaganda." Kompetenznetzwerk „Islamistischer Extremismus," Impuls No. 6, November 10, 2022, 5.
[14] See Heß 2023, 2.
[15] Ibid., 4.

Gulf states, as well as for Russian relations with Iran and Syria. Neither Saudi Arabia nor the UAE could be persuaded to openly support the American countermeasures in the days following the Russian invasion, thereby snubbing their traditional partner, the USA. Kadyrov is no stranger to other Arab states either. In many places, his Islamic-style propaganda about Russia is viewed with suspicion and rejection, but quite a few in the Middle East are receptive to his machismo posturing. Kadyrov's appearance certainly contributes to the fact that Putin can use anti-imperialist and post-colonial rhetoric in many Middle Eastern countries to present himself as a freedom fighter against American dominance and the Jewish president of Ukraine, who is supported by the West.[16] This supports a public opinion that is traditionally pro-Russian in some Islamic countries, is increasingly oriented towards Russia elsewhere, or sees Russia as a welcome player for balancing Western influence in a given country.[17]

4. Islam in the Russian war of aggression

4.1 Stability and control

Since the establishment of the OMSA and the muftiates, Russian Islam policy has served to secure stability and control over the politically most important religious minority in the country. Especially in times of crisis, this control is of considerable importance for the Russian regime.[18] Through conservative rhetoric and an active Islam policy, Moscow has so far managed to turn the majority of Russian Muslims into allies in the war of aggression against Ukraine. However, the gradual assimilation and subordination of the muftiates and of Russian Islam in general to the state and the ROC could

---

16 See Kashan, Hilal. "Auf der Suche nach dem neuen Saladin: Unterstützung für Putin in der arabischen Welt." Cicero Online, April 12, 2022. https://www.cicero.de/aussenpolitik/unterstutzung-fur-putin-in-der-arabischen-welt-auf-der-suche-nach-neuen-helden.
17 See Laruelle 2023, 17.
18 See Laruelle 2023, 28.

also become a problem due to the muftiates' low theological legitimacy.[19]

4.2 Legitimization and alliance building

Immediately after the start of the Russian war of aggression against Ukraine, numerous Muslim authorities sought to legitimize the invasion in Islamic terms. The Chechen mufti Salakh Mezhiev declared the attack a "jihad for the prophet and Islam" and a group of muftis from other parts of the country declared those killed in the war to be Islamic martyrs in a legal opinion (fatwa) shortly afterwards.[20] As described above, the "jihad narrative" is very popular with Muslims at home and abroad and contributes, at least to a certain extent, to the legitimization of war and the formation of alliances. But these argumentation patterns are less effective among jihadists and Islamist terrorists. Here, the prevailing belief is that it is in the interests of Islam if "the oppressors" (Russia and the West) destroy each other.[21] The dangers of the appropriation of the "jihad narrative" by Russian officials became apparent in October 2022, when a group of Muslim soldiers allegedly shot at least 11 comrades in a dispute over the correct use of Islamic terms.[22]

4.3 Fighters and cannon fodder

The Russian army leadership preferred to send young men from the Muslim-dominated Russian peripheral regions to the front in Ukraine. Through this recruitment policy, the Russian regime was initially able to avoid a broad mobilization in the central parts of the country and keep the war away from the core Russian population for longer. The recruitment of Muslim minorities is explained in literature primarily by socioeconomic factors. However, it remains a matter of speculation whether this also intended to reduce

---

19 See Laruelle 2021, 31.
20 Cited after Kemper, Michael. "Ijtihad in Putin's Russia? Signature Fatwas from Moscow and Kazan." Journal of the Economic and Social History of the Orient 65 (2022), 936.
21 See Gaspar/Sold 2022, 4.
22 See Laruelle 2023, 11.

a potentially troublemaking population group that was "not missed by the majority of the population".[23]

4.4 Excursus: Ukrainian Islamic policy

Muslim fighters and Islamic religious propaganda also play a significant role on the Ukrainian side, as numerous Chechens have joined the Ukrainian troops out of hatred for Russia. Central Asians, Tartars and refugees from Russia's Turkic-speaking republics and former Syrian fighters and jihadists are also fighting on the Ukrainian side. The most important Muslim religious scholars in Ukraine have called for the country to be defended and are also using genuinely Islamic arguments to do so.[24] Finally, Kadyrov's opponents have also formed two battalions on the Ukrainian side. Observers therefore speak of a "proxy war".[25]

5. Conclusion

Russia's Islamic policy plays a crucial role in the war of aggression against Ukraine. It establishes ideological and religious legitimacy, secures social and political control, provides a framework for combating domestic political opponents, and supplies the armed forces with fighters. However, this policy also harbors risks. The exploitation of intra-Muslim rivalries is reviving ethnic and sectarian conflicts in Russia and attracting jihadist terrorists who see "Russian Islam" as blasphemy. Another significant aspect relevant to Western interests and politics is the unity of Russian nationalism and Islamic propaganda through strong anti-Western sentiments. This interferes with Western efforts to stabilize the post-Soviet and Middle Eastern regions.

---

23 Such assumptions can be found, for example, in Kasakow, Evgeniy. "Ukraine-Krieg: Russland mobilisiert den Superstar." nd Journalismus von links, November 3, 2023. https://www.nd-aktuell.de/artikel/1188961.ukraine-krieg-russland-mobilisiert-den-superstar.html.
24 Gaspar/Sold 2022, 5.
25 Heß 2023, 6.

Military Chaplaincy on the Front Line
Theological Practice in the Horror of War?

Regina Elsner

The role of religion in Russia's war of aggression in Ukraine is complex and will generate in-depth analysis in the coming years. One aspect that has rarely received attention and academic analysis is the presence of clergy in both armed forces. The institution of religious presence in the armed forces, known as military chaplaincy, is an important part of the military structure for both armies — in Ukraine and Russia — with partly similar characteristics, but also significant differences. Historically, the presence of the church in the army was a natural extension of the pre-modern connection between religion and state before the collapse of the monarchies at the beginning of the 20th century. In contrast, the secular or atheist systems have, since the beginning of the 20th century, pursued a more or less radical separation of church and state, so that religion had no place in the armed forces until the end of the Soviet Union. After the end of the Soviet Union, the armed forces as well as the role of religion in society and politics developed very differently in the two countries, which is part of a larger alienation that is ultimately also reflected in this war. In the following, the structures, content, and theological guidelines of military chaplaincy during the war will be presented and discussed.

Ukraine — Religious diversity and "spiritual security"

Since gaining independence in 1991, Ukraine has enforced extremely liberal religious legislation that protects and strengthens the country's religious diversity. As a legacy of Soviet religious policy, a certain degree of control over the religious landscape has been maintained to this day by a state religious office. However, this office primarily serves to properly register religious communities and to channel the communication between religious organizations and the state. The "All-Ukrainian Council of Churches and Religious

Communities" (AUCCRO), founded in 1996, was established to take over this function on the religious side. To this day, almost 95% of the country's organized religious communities are represented in the AUCCRO, which plays a key role in developing the framework for cooperation between the state and religious groups. As there is no legally privileged religious community in Ukraine that could make a special claim to a direct religious presence in state institutions, the formulation of the principles of military chaplaincy has also been one of the Council's responsibilities.

In the 1990s, there was initially sporadic cooperation between certain clergymen in individual units of the Ukrainian army. Most military units were given a small chapel or church where priests from nearby towns regularly celebrated services. These were primarily Orthodox churches of the largest and only established Orthodox church at the time, the Ukrainian Orthodox Church (UOC) in communion with the Moscow Patriarchate. Other religious communities—the Ukrainian Greek Catholic Church (UGCC), Protestant churches, and Muslim communities—visited units on a voluntary basis or provided humanitarian support as needed. In the 2000s, more coordinated cooperation began between the state authorities, particularly with the UOC and the Ukrainian Orthodox Church—Kyiv Patriarchate (UOC-KP), which was founded in 1992, as well as with the UGCC. All three churches set up special departments for cooperation with the armed forces.[1] There were also interdenominational and interreligious associations to strengthen the pastoral care of military personnel and institutional cooperation. Regular conferences discussed current challenges and supported professional networking. Nevertheless, the structure of the work remained the voluntary work of priests and other specially appointed persons. An official joint declaration between the Ministry of Defense and religious communities was not issued until 2008,

---

1 See Department for Military Chaplaincy UGKK. "Про нас" Oktober 2006. https://www.kapelanstvo.ugcc.ua/pro-nas/.

followed by several legislative initiatives, which, however, repeatedly failed.²

In 2009, an interreligious council for the pastoral care of military personnel was established in the Ministry of Defense. Thanks to its international network, the UGCC was able to contribute important experience and expertise to the development of a sustainable apparatus for military chaplaincy and became a key player in drafting legislation.

The annexation of Crimea by Russia and the start of the hybrid war in eastern Ukraine in the spring of 2014 changed the dynamic, leading to the professionalization of military chaplaincy and the development of a separate law that would not only support soldiers and enable them to exercise their religious freedom but also provide chaplains with social security.

This law "On the Service of the Military Chaplaincy"³ was finally passed in the fall of 2021 and came into force in the fall of 2022 — after the full-scale invasion of the Russian army. It regulates the rank and training of chaplains — a higher theological degree is required — the quota for certain religious representatives, and the scope of the military chaplaincy.

As Synchak, Livak and Fedorenko note, military chaplaincy developed in parallel with the democratic awakening of Ukrainian society.⁴ It is noteworthy that respect for freedom of religion and conscience is the top priority in all documents on military chaplaincy, followed by questions of ethical support for the armed

---

2   See Козак, Оксана. "Бути поруч завжди»: значення і подробиці закону про військових капеланів в Україні." Dezember 14, 2021. https://ugcc.ua/data/buty-poruch-zavzhdy-znachennya-i-podrobytsi-zakonu-pro-viyskovyh-kapelaniv-v-ukrayni-417/.

3   The law can be found on the homepage of the Ukrainian parliament: See Інформаційне управління Апарату Верховної Ради України. "Прийнято Закон ›Про Службу військового капеланства‹." November 30, 2021. https://www.rada.gov.ua/news/Novyny/217100.html. Text and edits of the law: "Проект Закону про Службу військового капеланства." January 22, 2021. https://w1.c1.rada.gov.ua/pls/zweb2/webproc4_1?pf3511=70878.

4   See Synchak, Bogdan, Petro Livak, und Mykhailo Fedorenko. "Training of Military Chaplains for the Armed Forces of Ukraine in Conditions of the Invasion by the Russian Federation." *Occasional Papers on Religion in Eastern Europe* 42 (2022). https://doi.org/10.55221/2693-2148.2345.

forces. In the law, the principles include: 1) recognition of constitutional freedom of religion; 2) equal rights for all faiths; 3) equal rights for all chaplains regardless of their faith community; 4) tolerant treatment of other chaplains; 5) prohibition of proselytism; 6) voluntary participation in religious offerings; 7) priority of military tasks over spiritual-religious needs. The tasks attributed to the military chaplaincy include: 1) enabling the exercise of religious needs; 2) developing collective morale; 3) popularizing a healthy lifestyle; 4) strengthening ideological tolerance; 5) establishing contacts with other religious representatives in places of military posting; 6) providing rehabilitation support and psychological assistance; 7) advising commanders on religious issues. Chaplains are prohibited from using weapons and ammunition.

The focus on human rights and the practical absence of the patriotic interests of the country or the armed forces as an expectation of the religious communities is particularly significant in comparison with the development of military chaplaincy in Russia and the departure from the Soviet concepts of the ideological education of servicemen and women.

This emphasis on human rights aligns with the religious and ideological diversity in Ukraine, which has been restored and supported as a special value since the end of the Soviet Union. It also reflects the fundamentally democratic development of society and the state since 2004. The need for such a foundation in the armed forces was particularly underscored by the active participation of all religious communities in the "Revolution of Dignity" in 2013/14. There, religious communities—especially Christian churches—demonstrated their de-escalating potential and the broad social recognition of their moral authority, which ultimately also had an impact on the strong references to human dignity among the demonstrators. Continuing this legacy, in 2017 the religious communities published a joint "Strategy for the Participation of Ukrainian Religious Communities in the Peace Process" through the AUCCRO. This strategy is intended to serve as a peace ethics framework during wartime, with the armed forces described as defenders of peaceful coexistence, whose real goal is peace.[5]

Religiosity among the Ukrainian population remains high, meaning that there is also a great need for pastoral care within the armed forces. At the same time, there is a general lack of comprehensive psychological support, especially given the extremely brutal and traumatizing nature of the Russian war of aggression. The number of chaplains at the front remains low; of the almost 740 positions allocated by law, only around 80 were permanently filled in 2023. Several hundred future chaplains are in training, and many are still working on a voluntary basis at the front, primarily in hospitals and with families. Experienced military chaplains, such as the Greek-Catholic Andrij Zelinskij, are striving for good networking in further training and better psychological support for military chaplains and military personnel in this war.

The military chaplaincy's public reports from the front are generally rather reserved, characterized by compassion for the combatants and their families as well as for their spiritual and psychological conflicts.

Despite the great importance attached by law to ideological tolerance in military chaplaincy, the debates surrounding the country's "spiritual independence" during the Russian war of aggression have had an impact on interreligious coexistence. The debate about the security risk that could emanate from the Ukrainian Orthodox Church (UOC), which had links to the Russian Orthodox Church, came to a head with the open war of aggression and ultimately led to a controversial discussion in 2023 about banning this church. Nonetheless, a significant proportion of soldiers are committed to the UOC, and UOC parishes are involved in supporting the army, including voluntary military chaplaincy. The access of UOC clergy to the armed forces, especially on the direct front, was already becoming increasingly difficult before 2022, largely depending on

---

5   See UCCRO. "Strategy for Participation of Ukrainian Religious Organizations in the Peacebuilding Process." Dezember 10, 2017. https://vrciro.ua/en/documents/uccro-peacebuilding-strategy-ukraine.

personal, trust-based relationships between commanders, and certain priests. However, after corresponding changes are made to the Religion Act and the Military Chaplaincy Act in 2024, this access became impossible for the time being, which poses a limitation to the religious freedom of faithful military personnel.

Russia: Militarisation and theology of war

The Russian development of the concept of military chaplaincy differs fundamentally from the Ukrainian development. This is primarily caused by two factors: Firstly, democratic development, particularly regarding religious freedom, was slowed down at the latest with the 1997 law on religion and the privileged status of the Russian Orthodox Church (ROC) in its cooperation with state structures. Secondly, repressive domestic policies from 2011 onwards have reinforced this trend across various sectors of society. In line with this political and social development, an extremely close cooperation between the armed forces and the ROC has developed in Russia. As in other areas of state-church cooperation, patriotic and "spiritual-cultural"[6] education is prioritized by representatives of the church. This ideological focus is a paradigm of victory, which defines victory over Nazi Germany in the Second World War as a central feature of the identity of the current Russian Federation and thus promotes the sacralization of the Russian army as the direct successor to the Soviet army. This sacralization and militarization culminated in the inauguration of the main cathedral of the Armed Forces of the Russian Federation near Moscow in May 2020.[7]

This concept is made particularly destructive by the systematic disregard for human dignity within military structures, which

---

[6] The most recent reference was made in March 2024, when Patriarch Kirill and Victor Zolotov, general of the National Guard, signed a new agreement of collaboration of both institutions: see "Состоялось подписание Соглашения о сотрудничестве между Русской Православной Церковью и Федеральной службой войск национальной гвардии." March 14, 2024. http://www.patriarchia.ru/db/text/6111564.html.

[7] See Golovko, Oksana. "В стиле советского плаката. Искусствоведы, священник и иконописец — о храме Вооруженных сил России." May 1, 2020. https://www.pravmir.ru/v-stile-sovetskogo-plakata-iskusstvovedy-svyashhennik-i-ikonopisecz-o-hrame-vooruzhennyh-sil-rossii/.

has led to an unmanageable abundance of abuse of power, sexual abuse, increased suicidal tendencies and secondary illnesses — above all addiction and depression — among conscripts and professional soldiers since the end of the Soviet Union. Since the 1990s, the ROC has been the only religious community with nationwide access to military units. In 1994, joint structures were established between the ROC and the Ministry of Defense, and several conferences addressed the tradition of cooperation between the Russian army and the Orthodox Church, as well as the "spiritual, moral and Orthodox traditions of the Russian army".[8] In the years that followed, the ROC intensified its cooperation with the military, especially under the then Metropolitan Kirill (Gundjaev), leading to the consecration of specially built churches, the canonization of certain military leaders from Russian history and the special blessing of warships and weapons carriers, including nuclear weapons. Even though the institute of military chaplaincy was only introduced by the Ministry of Defense in 2009, priests were already regularly present in all structures.

From the ROC's first initiatives in the early 1990s, the focus of military chaplaincy was on the patriotic and moral education of soldiers and the restoration of the Orthodox tradition within the armed forces. No references were made to the human right to freedom of religion and belief or to humane treatment within the military. In 2013, the Synod of the ROC adopted the "Regulations for the Military Clergy of the Russian Orthodox Church in the Russian Federation", which describe the duties of military clergy as follows: 1) conducting divine services and religious rites; 2) spiritual and educational work; 3) participation in the activities carried out by the command for the patriotic and moral education of soldiers (personnel) and their family members; 4) assisting the command in the implementation of preventive measures to strengthen public order and discipline, prevent criminal offenses, unlawful relations and suicidal incidents; 5) advising the command on religious issues; 6)

---

8   See Lukichev, Boris. "Патриарх Кирилл и военное духовенство." June 2015. https://old.pobeda.ru/wp-content/uploads/2018/12/Patriarh-Kirill-i-voennoe-duhovenstvo-poslednyaya-redaktsiya-28.06.2015.pdf.

participating in the formation of collective relations based on the norms of Christian morality; 7) participating in the formation of a healthy moral climate in the families of soldiers.[9] Issues of pastoral or psychological support for soldiers, or the protection of human rights, are not mentioned in the text, nor is the topic of peace or compliance with certain standards of humane treatment in war or conflict situations. Service to the fatherland, which is associated with the constant willingness to sacrifice oneself, thus becomes the fundamental element of military chaplaincy.

As in Ukraine, the war on the neighboring country has accelerated the dynamics of military chaplaincy in Russia, but it is striking that this already began in 2013. In the years before 2022, there was a problematic link between Russia's paramilitary activities through the Wagner mercenary group in Africa and the expansion of ROC structures, which was confirmed in 2022 and 2023 by the opaque relations between the exarch for Russian church structures, Leonid (Gorbachev), and the leader of the Wagner group, Yevgeny Prigozhin. During the war of aggression against Ukraine, the church leadership fully supported the ideology of war as a defense of its own civilizational space against evil forces. Military chaplaincy is, therefore, in its self-understanding a reinforcement of the armed forces in their self-sacrificing service, which the head of the church confirmed in his sermon of September 25, 2022, by referring to the "salvific sacrifice"[10].

Accessible reports about the clergy at the front are largely characterized by a determined will to win and the symbolism of the struggle against fascism, evil, and the enemy. In addition to the regular military chaplains, there are also numerous volunteers in-

---

9   See "Положение о военном духовенстве Русской Православной Церкви в Российской Федерации." December 26, 2013. http://www.patriarchia.ru/db/text/3481010.html.
10 "Патриаршая проповедь в Неделю 15-ю по Пятидесятнице после Литургии в Александро-Невском скиту." September 25, 2022. http://www.patriarchia.ru/db/text/5962628.html.

volved in direct combat operations, who do not face the punishments stipulated by church regulations.[11] Many priests have also died in combat.[12]

Before the Russian invasion of Ukraine, neither the ROC nor the Department for Cooperation with the Armed Forces took a position on the inhumane conditions in the army or the excessive violence of the Russian military in Ukraine. The proven crimes against humanity committed by members of the Russian army are not addressed at any point in church statements, which must be seen as a moral failure. Russian Orthodox priests are at least aware of the circumstances surrounding the filtration camps in the occupied territories and the mass deportation of Ukrainian children, if not directly involved. The participation of the ROC in the war crimes of the Russian army, whether through military chaplains or voluntary participation of clergy, will require not only an examination under international law but also its own theological reappraisal in the context of ecumenical peace ethics.

Conclusion

The practice of military chaplaincy in Russia's war against Ukraine is a strong illustration of the contrasting attitudes to the religions involved in this specific war and to warfare as a whole. While Ukrainian religious communities and the Ministry of Defense have been persuaded by civil society to take a democratic approach to cooperation since the Orange Revolution, a militaristic interplay between autocracy and Orthodoxy has developed in Russia. Military chaplaincy in Ukraine sees itself as a multi- and inter-religious support for members of the armed forces in recognition of their human and service challenges and as a guarantor of respect for fundamental human rights. In contrast, Russian military chaplaincy supports an exclusive Orthodox patriotism and, considering the war in

---

11   See Pronina, Karina. "Если священник взял в руки оружие, это ни о чём не говорит." September 10, 2023. https://baikal-journal.ru/2023/09/10/esli-sv yashhennik-vzyal-v-ruki-oruzhie-eto-ni-o-chyom-ne-govorit/.

12   See also the monitoring by the Belarussian group „Christians against War": "Христиане против войны. Священники РПЦ на фронте." Oktober 28, 2023. https://shaltnotkill.info/svyashhenniki-rpcz-na-fronte/.

Ukraine, even an imperialistic ideology that does not shy away from the myth of salutary self-sacrifice. In addition to the humanitarian catastrophe that this war is causing, it also means a massive ethical and theological rupture between two predominantly Christian societies.

'Just War' and 'Emergency Aid'
Obsolete or Key Categories for the War in Ukraine?

Franz-Josef Bormann

Russia's war of aggression against Ukraine, which violated international law and did not just begin on February 24, 2022, but reached its first climax in 2014 with the annexation of Crimea, has often been described as a historic caesura. While Federal Chancellor Olaf Scholz spoke of a 'turning point' (Zeitenwende) in his much-noticed speech in the German Bundestag on February 27, 2022, Federal President Frank-Walter Steinmeier soon afterward described it as a veritable 'epochal break'[1]. Although this vocabulary may be exaggerated, it is correct that there is now finally a growing willingness across party lines within German politics to critically reassess previous patterns of perception and, above all, to correct the wrong defense policy decisions of recent decades, which have resulted in a fatal weakening of Germany's defense capability. However, not only the Federal Government, but also the leading bodies of the Christian churches are called upon to self-critically rethink their recent peace-ethics positions and to update them to do justice to the current challenges.[2]

---

1 See Bundespräsident Frank-Walter Steinmeier. „Bei der Eröffnung des 22. Ordentlichen Bundeskongresses des Deutschen Gewerkschaftsbundes." May 8, 2022. https://www.bundespraesident.de/SharedDocs/Reden/DE/Frank-Walter-Steinmeier/Reden/2022/05/220508-DGB-Bundeskongress.html.

2 For the following remarks see Bormann, Franz-Josef. „Eine ‚Zeitenwende' auch für die katholische Friedenslehre? Moraltheologische Überlegungen zum russischen Angriffskrieg auf die Ukraine." Theologische Quartalschrift 51, Nr. 3 (2023): 25–43.

1. The complexity of the biblical findings and the theological tradition

The widespread idea that the contribution of the Christian religion to security policy matters is exhausted in a pacifist utopia, which appears to be ethically respectable but proves to be of little use in dealing with real political problems, does not do justice to the complexity of biblical textual evidence or the multilayered nature of the theological tradition. The Old Testament shows an astonishing variability on war and peace depending on the changed political constitution of ancient Israel.[3] This ranges from the justification of wars of aggression and the exaggeration of warlike actions, to so-called 'holy wars', to the prophetic warning of hopeless warlike uprisings against neighboring great powers to which Israel was subject as a vassal state, as well as distinctly pacifist visions, especially in the most recent text formations. These texts were created under post-state conditions, and due to their strongly eschatological coloring, do not represent direct political instructions for action, but rather evoke images of hope that fulfill originally religious functions.

In the New Testament, Jesus' statements on renouncing violence and loving one's enemies in the Sermon on the Mount contain a clear trace of criticism of violence, obliging all Christians to adopt an attitude of forgiveness and to overcome the everyday spiral of violence to bear credible witness to the dawn of God's kingdom. But these instructions are primarily related to the personal dealing with individual opponents. In contrast, a direct transfer to the political sphere — particularly to the actions of a modern secular, religiously and ideologically neutral state — is likely beyond the scope of these texts.[4] Nevertheless, this does not weaken the obligation of

---

[3] See Lohfink, Norbert. Krieg und Staat im alten Israel. Beiträge zur Friedensethik 14. Barsbüttel, 1992, Krochmalnik, Daniel. „Krieg und Frieden in der hebräischen Bibel und rabbinischen Tradition." In Handbuch Friedensethik, herausgegeben von Ines-Jacqueline Werkner und Klaus Ebeling, Wiesbaden, 2017, 191–202.

[4] This finding must be carefully distinguished from the various attempts at interpretation based on professional ethics, interim ethics or ethical convictions which have been developed in the course of the history of theology and which have led to a reduction of the meaning of the highly ethical instructions of the

individual Christians to work for the peaceful coexistence of peoples beyond their private environment. It merely reminds us that several levels of responsibility must be distinguished from one another within a political community, marking functionally differentiated responsibilities despite the many interactions and interdependencies. It is, therefore, hardly surprising that a variety of different positions can be found in the long history of Christian-inspired peace ethics, depending on the historical constellation and the primary addressees.

2. The traditional doctrine of *ius ad bellum* and *ius in bello*

For reasons of coherence alone, church statements on war and peace should ensure that the basic insights of their own tradition are appropriately emphasized. Although it would be a complete misunderstanding of the actual genesis of Christian peace ethics to conceive it as a rigid canon of unchanging principles and to ignore the historical dimension of insight into many thematic and normative growths in its doctrinal content, this does not mean, conversely, that there are no lines of continuity at all. This can be illustrated by the traditional doctrine of *ius ad bellum* and *ius in bello*, which has had a lasting influence on the development of international humanitarian law of war.

Three objections are usually raised against this doctrine: Firstly, it stems from a time when there was no comprehensive prohibition of the use of force under international law and when war was still fundamentally regarded as a legitimate means of politics, which is no longer the case. Secondly, technological innovations—

Sermon on the Mount; see Fürst, Alfons. „Friedensethik und Gewaltbereitschaft. Zur Ambivalenz des christlichen Monotheismus in seinen Anfängen." In Frieden auf Erden? Die Weltreligionen zwischen Gewaltverzicht und Gewaltbereitschaft, herausgegeben von Alfons Fürst, Freiburg, 2006, 45–81; Hengel, Martin. „Gewalt und Gewaltlosigkeit. Zur ‚Politischen Theologie' in neutestamentlicher Zeit." In Jesus und die Evangelien. Kleine Schriften 5 (WUNT 211), Tübingen, 2007, 245–288. and Luz, Ulrich. „Feindesliebe und Gewaltverzicht: Zur Struktur und Problematik neutestamentlicher Friedensideen." In Krieg und Christentum. Religiöse Gewalttheorien in der Kriegserfahrung des Westens, herausgegeben von Andreas Holzem, Paderborn, 2009, 137–149.

in particular the development of modern NBC weapons — have now led to a situation where a strict distinction between combatants and non-combatants is no longer possible and the relevant authorization and prohibition criteria can therefore no longer be applied. Thirdly, this doctrine does not do justice to the new challenges posed by hybrid forms of warfare, civil war-like unrest in the context of so-called failing states, and terrorist threats, as it is conceptually rooted in the model of inter-state war scenarios. Although all these concerns should be taken seriously, they do not justify a general rejection of the *just war* doctrine, either individually or collectively, for two reasons.[5]

On the one hand, the attempts to construct a contrast between the supposedly new model of a 'just peace' and the traditional *bellum iustum* doctrine are based on the false assumption of a normative dissent in the target perspective, which is proven to be wrong on closer inspection. Since the doctrine of just war "is not primarily concerned with justifying the use of military means, but with securing peace and preventing war, or limiting it where it cannot be prevented"[6], there is no fundamental teleological difference between the two concepts. On the other hand, the traditional criteria for examining the legitimacy of the use of military force are still highly relevant and indispensable today. Thomas of Aquinas traces the criteria back to the classical triad: firstly, to the formal authority of the political leadership of a community (in the sense of *auctoritas principis*); secondly, to the just cause existing in grave injustice (in the sense of *causa iusta*); thirdly, the right intention to secure peace (in the sense of *recta intentio*).[7] The current World Catechism also lists the *ultima ratio* condition, the realistic prospect of success and the proportionality requirement as part of a harm-benefit assessment.[8] Irrespective of these differences in detail, it is always a matter of formulating demanding requirements to justify the use of armed

---

5   See Spieker, Manfred. „Christliche Friedensethik und der Krieg in der Ukraine. Warum die Lehre vom gerechten Krieg nicht überholt ist." IkZ Communio 51, Nr. 5 (2022): 557–569.
6   Ibid, 560.
7   See Thomas von Aquin. STh II II q. 40 a.1.
8   See Katechismus der Katholischen Kirche. Nr. 2309. Leipzig, 2019.

forces in the first place. Such criteria are needed in the context of the debate on so-called humanitarian interventions (in the sense of a *responsibility to protect*)[9] as well as in the context of classic interstate conflicts, which can also be expected in the future. If these criteria are applied to the current war in Ukraine, the Russian attack on Ukraine—a sovereign state since 1991—fulfills all the criteria of an unjust war. Conversely, Ukraine has every moral right to defend itself against the aggressor to protect the lives and the right to self-determination of its population as well as the integrity of the state. The ethical significance of this insight is not diminished by the fact that the Church's position has evolved in recent years towards a more comprehensive concept of 'just peace', which pays significantly more attention to the prevention of violence in its social, economic, human rights and ecological dimensions.[10]

As important as it is to foresee possible causes of war and to prevent armed conflicts from breaking out in the first place, it remains necessary to consistently apply the proven criteria for identifying justified forms of the use of force in the 21st century wherever fundamental rights of victims of violence are disregarded. Therefore, it is wrong to set up an opposition between the doctrine of *just war* and the concept of *just peace*, and to play the two approaches off against each other, as has regrettably occurred not only in some prominent positions of the Protestant Church[11], but also in individual statements by Pope Francis in recent times.[12] The concept of *just peace* is neither a contradiction nor an alternative to the

---

9 See Laukötter, Sebastian. Zwischen Einmischung und Nothilfe. Das Problem der „humanitären Intervention" aus völkerrechtlicher Perspektive. Quellen und Studien zur Philosophie 116. Berlin/Boston, 2014.
10 See Die deutschen Bischöfe. Gerechter Friede. 2013 (4th ed.). https://www.dbk -shop.de/media/files_public/aa854b8461836b577d6a6d8d6d7278f6/DBK_11 66.pdf, part II.2.
11 See Bedford-Strohm, Heinrich. „Gerechter Friede und militärische Gewalt. Friedensethische Überlegungen im Lichte des Angriffskrieges gegen die Ukraine." Herder-Korrespondenz 76, Nr. 5 (2022): 13–16 and more cautiously Kurschus, Annette. „Jenseits von Eden." Frankfurter Allgemeine Zeitung, June 7, 2022, Nr. 130, 7.
12 See Franziskus. Enzyklika Fratelli tutti (3. October 2020). Acta Apostolicae Sedis 112 (2020), Nr. 258.

traditional doctrine of *just war*, but rather describes a complementary perspective that supplements the proven concept of *bellum iustum* by incorporating important elements of a violence-preventive policy. In contrast, the invocation of a supposedly Christian pacifism, which fundamentally refuses to speak of 'just wars' and to name the true causes of a real armed conflict, not only runs the risk of falling behind the differentiation of traditional conceptual distinctions, but also leads to logical and conceptual contradictions,[13] which ultimately unintentionally play into the hands of aggressors.

3. The meaning of self-defense and emergency aid

As it is well known, the Catholic Church has always defended the right to life of every innocent human being at all stages of their existence as a fundamental good that eludes all purely utilitarian calculations and marks an unconditional deontological boundary for all processes of consideration. From the basic right to life follows a moral right to self-defense against unjust aggressors, which can also be extended to collective actors. Although hardly anyone denied the Ukrainian people the fundamental right to defend themselves against the Russian attack by force of arms, there were voices, which repeatedly advocated for an end to the bloodshed through quick negotiations considering the military power imbalance between the aggressor and the victim of violence — even if this meant not only the cession of considerable parts of Ukrainian territory, but also the de facto capitulation to the obvious breach of elementary international law provisions. The main problem with this position was that it reduced the decision-making space to two equally unsatisfactory alternatives: either waging a hopeless war with high casualty figures or accepting a Russian-dictated peace. The suggestion by some German intellectuals to recommend the second option to the Ukrainians from a safe distance as the soberly calculated *minus malum* was in danger of being (mis)understood as

---

13 See Steinhoff, Uwe. „Gerechtigkeit kann schrecklich sein. Friedensethik hilft hier nicht weiter: Prüfkriterien für den gerechten Krieg." Frankfurter Allgemeine Zeitung, April 23, 2022, Nr. 94, 9.

a presumptuous gesture that could too obviously conceal their own interests. More importantly, this strategy ignored the question of whether self-stylization as a seemingly uninvolved observer was not bought at the price of ignoring irreducible personal responsibilities. This raises difficult questions for Western democracies about the existence and scope of specific obligations of third parties to provide assistance. Although they are not directly attacked, they are certainly in a position to provide effective assistance to the victims of violence.[14] To avoid the diffusion of responsibility in such constellations, the moral theological tradition has developed two concepts of thought which, although originating in individual ethics, can also be applied *mutatis mutandis* in collective action.

One concept relates to the so-called *ordo caritatis*, according to which the nature and extent of our respective positive duties depend largely on the social relationships and geographical proximity between the relevant actors. Irrespective of the universality of fundamental and human rights, which everyone is obliged to respect always and everywhere without exception, there is a graduated responsibility that increases with growing proximity. Even if it is unjustified to play off the necessary support for Ukraine, which is currently neither a member of NATO nor the EU, against the various out-of-area deployments of the German armed forces within the framework of existing alliance commitments, the Russian attack on a neighboring Eastern European country does affect the entire European security architecture to a great extent. It would, therefore, be strange if we wanted to defend German interests in the Hindu Kush while continuing to marginalize our much greater responsibility towards our Eastern European neighbors.

The other relevant concept is the doctrine of 'cooperation in evil' (*cooperatio ad malum*), which includes both culpable omission and active support for unlawful acts. Anyone who can help a victim of violence but either decides not to provide help or fails to decide (in time) to provide the necessary help is complicit in the criminal

---

14 It is therefore not only a question of the permissibility of such assistance in the sense of its moral possibility, but also of its imperative in the sense of its moral necessity.

actions of third parties. Since the traditional doctrine of cooperation is sometimes criticized for focusing too much on the forms of cooperation between natural persons and ignoring the far more complex relationships between collective actors,[15] the war in Ukraine offers a good opportunity to correct this one-sidedness and explicitly include the collective level of responsibility of entire states in the analysis.

Although Germany, in close coordination with its European partners and the USA, attempted not only to exert political pressure on the Russian regime with several packages of sanctions, but also to strengthen its defense capabilities by supplying Ukraine with extensive arms, the German government's hesitant approach to the issue of arms deliveries, which was characterized by growing internal dissonance, was criticized, especially in the first months of the war. Not only was it in danger of leading to a loss of Germany's international reputation among its Western allies, but it was also increasingly failing to achieve the very security policy goals that it claimed to achieve by thwarting Russia's annexation plans. Although NATO states may not become a direct party to the war considering that they operate with their own personnel on Ukrainian territory, there is a moral obligation to do everything possible, irrespective of alliance-related rules of assistance, to enable the victim of violence to put up effective resistance within the limits of proportionality. This also includes the delivery of all types of so-called 'heavy weapons', as long as they are suitable for achieving the legitimate national defense objectives of the victim of aggression. The recurring debate about possible 'red lines' for each type of weapon may be politically understandable regarding internal party sensitivities – beyond all technical-operational questions – but it is likely to prove ethically unnecessary and counterproductive from a military-strategic point of view. Should it no longer be possible to persuade the Russian regime under Putin to permanently abandon its

---

15   See Rosenberger, Michael. „Reichweite und Stellenwert einer zeitgemäßen Lehre der Cooperatio." In Ein Pakt mit dem Bösen? Die moraltheologische Lehre der ‚cooperatio ad malum' und ihre Bedeutung heute, herausgegeben von Michael Rosenberger und Walter Schaupp, Münster, 2015, 77–89, especially, 81.

annexation plans through massive military resistance and to reconquer the Russian-occupied territories in a timely manner due to the initially too hesitant and gradually decreasing support from the West after the war has lasted almost three years, this would not only have fatal consequences for the possibility of quickly ending the current military confrontation through negotiated outcomes in accordance with international law, but also motivate Russia to embark on further military adventures in other 'breakaway Soviet republics' and thus further destabilizing the global security situation as a whole.

On the Contributors

Franz-Josef Bormann
Prof. Dr. Franz-Josef Bormann studied philosophy and Catholic theology in Frankfurt, Munich and Rome. Since 2008, he has been a professor of moral theology at the Catholic Theological Faculty at the University of Tübingen. From 2005 to 2008, he held a professorship for ethics and moral theology in Paderborn. From 2016-2024 he was a member of the German Ethics Council (DER). His book publications include *Nature as a Horizon of Moral Practice* (1999), *Social Justice between Fairness and Participation* (2006), *Conscience* (2014), *Life-Ending Actions* (2017), *Death and Dying* (2023). His articles have been published in the journals "Theology and Philosophy", "Theological Quarterly", "Communio", "Journal for Medical Ethics", "Voices of Time" and "The Political Opinion", among others.

Thomas Bremer
Prof. i.R. Dr. Thomas Bremer studied Catholic Theology, Slavistics, and Classical Philology in Munich, Belgrade, and Münster. From 1999 until 2022 he was professor of Ecumenics, Eastern Churches Studies, and Peace Studies at the Faculty of Catholic Theology at the University of Münster, Germany. After his dissertation in 1990, he worked there as a research assistant and between 1995 and 1999 as the Executive Director of the German Association of East European Studies. Among Bremer's most important publications are *Cross and Kremlin. A Brief History of the Orthodox* (2013), *Churches in the Ukrainian Crisis* (ed., 2017), *Orthodoxy in Two Manifestations? The Conflict in Ukraine as Expression of a Fault Line in World Orthodoxy* (ed., 2022).

Regina Elsner
Prof. Dr. Regina Elsner studied Catholic theology in Berlin and Münster. She has been Professor of Eastern Church Studies and Ecumenics at the Ecumenical Institute of the Faculty of Catholic Theology in Münster since 2024. Previously, Elsner worked as a re-

search assistant at the Centre for Eastern European and International Studies ZOiS in Berlin and as a project coordinator for Caritas Russia in St. Petersburg. Elsner is co-spokesperson of the Religion Section of the German Association for East European Studies (DGO e.V.), advisor to the Ecumenical Commission of the German Bishops' Conference and member of the German Commission for Justice and Peace. Her most recent publication is *The Russian Orthodox Church and Modernity A Historical and Theological Investigation into Eastern Christianity between Unity and Plurality* (2021). Her publications have appeared in "Religion, State and Society", "Nationalities Papers", "Osteuropa", "Review of Faith and International Affairs" and "European Theology Studies", among others, as well as numerous edited volumes.

Pinchas Goldschmidt
Chief Rabbi Pinchas Goldschmidt studied at the Ponevezh Yeshiva, the Telshe Yeshiva, Chicago, the Shevet Umechokek Institute for Rabbinical Judges and the Harry Fischel Institute for Talmudic Research, Jerusalem, Israel, and is an ordained rabbi. In addition to his rabbinical ordination, Goldschmidt holds an MA from Ner Israel Rabbinical College and an M.S. from Johns Hopkins University, both in Baltimore. In 2002, Goldschmidt was certified by the Chief Rabbinate of Israel as qualified for the position of Chief Rabbi in any Israeli city. He has been the President of the European Rabbinical Conference since 2011. In spring 2009, Goldschmidt was a visiting scholar at the Davis Centre for Russian and Eurasian Studies at Harvard University. Chief Rabbi Goldschmidt has been a visiting professor at TUM Munich since 2024.

Goldschmidt wrote articles on post-Soviet Jewry in the field of religious law and has spoken in the press and before international bodies such as the United States Senate, the European Parliament, the Council of Europe, the Knesset, Prime Minister Benjamin Netanyahu's Neeman Commission, Oxford University, the OSCE Berlin Conference on Anti-Semitism and Harvard University on current issues, mostly on the state of the Jewish community and the threats posed by anti-Semitism. His previous books include *Communitati et Orbi – To the Community and to the World* (May Editions, 2017), in German as *An die Gemeinschaft und an die Welt* (2018).

Oleksandr Geychenko

Dr. Oleksandr Geychenko studied Theology at the University of St Andrews, UK. He is the Rector of Odesa Theological Seminary in Odesa, Ukraine since 2018 and is also a member of the Editorial Board of the Series Contemporary Protestant Thought published by Eastern European Institute of Theology. Previously, Geychenko was Vice-President of Euro-Asian Accrediting Association. He is a member of European Baptist Federation Theology and Education Committee. He is the author of *Brotherhood in Christ: Towards a Ukrainian Baptist Perspective on Associations of Churches* (2024). His papers have been published, among others, by "International Journal of Public Theology" and "Baptist Quarterly".

Andreas Heinemann-Grüder

Prof. Dr. Andreas Heinemann-Grüder studied history, political science and German literature at the Free University of Berlin and joined a post-graduate program at the Lomonosov University in Moscow. He has been teaching political science at the University of Bonn since 2006 and is a senior fellow at CASSIS there and at the Global Public Policy Institute in Berlin. His previous positions include the Berghof Institute Berlin (1989-92), Humboldt University Berlin (1993-95), Duke University (1995), University of Pennsylvania (1996-99), University of Cologne (2002-2005) and the Bonn International Centre for Conflict Studies (1999-2024). His book publications include "Who are the Fighters? Irregular Armed Groups in the Russia-Ukrainian War since 2014" (hg., 2024), "Lehren aus dem Ukrainekonflikt. Krisen vorbeugen, Gewalt verhindern" (hg. with Claudia Crawford, Tim B. Peters, 2022) and "Osteuropa zwischen Mauerfall und Ukrainekrieg. Besichtigung einer Epoche" (with Angelika Nußberger, Martin Aust, Ulrich Schmid, 2022).

Andreas Jacobs

Dr. Andreas Jacobs studied Political Science, Middle Eastern Studies and German literature in Cologne, Tunis and Cairo. Since 2024 he is the Deputy Head of the Analysis and Consulting Division at the Konrad Adenauer Foundation in Berlin. He also heads the social cohesion department of the foundation. Between 2013 and 2017 he worked as a Research Advisor at the NATO Defense College in Rome. From 2007 to 2012 he headed the office of the Konrad Adenauer Foundation in Cairo, Egypt. Andreas Jacobs is a founding member of the Expert Initiative on Religious Policy (EIR) and a member of the advisory board of the Protestant Centre for Religious and Ideological Issues (EZW). He authored numerous publications on Islam, religious politics, the Middle East and security policy.

Johannes Oeldemann

Dr. Johannes Oeldemann studied Catholic theology and Slavic studies at the universities of Münster and Tübingen. He has been Director of the Johann Adam Moehler Institute for Ecumenism in Paderborn since 2001. He previously worked as a research assistant at the Ecumenical Institute of the Faculty of Catholic Theology in Münster and as a referent at Renovabis, the solidarity campaign of German Catholics with people in Central and Eastern Europe, in Freising. Dr. Oeldemann is a member of the Faith and Order Commission of the World Council of Churches, an advisor to the Ecumenical Commission of the German Catholic Bishops' Conference and a member of several Orthodox-Catholic dialogue commissions at national and international level. His publications include a book on *The Churches of the Christian East*, which has appeared in several editions, an introduction to ecumenical theology and a study of Christian denominations. His articles have been published in "Herder Korrespondenz", "Stimmen der Zeit", "Ökumenische Rundschau", "Ostkirchliche Studien", "Catholica", "Communio", "Orthodoxes Forum", and the online magazine "Religions".

Ludwig Ring-Eifel

Ludwig Ring-Eifel studied Philosophy, Theology, Religious Studies, Classical Philology and Public Law in Trier, Santa Barbara and

Mainz. He is senior correspondent with the KNA news agency and their bureau chief in Rome. From 2005 thru 2022 he was KNA's chief editor. His previous books include *Weltmacht Vatikan* (2004) and *Johannes Paul II.* (2005).

Joshua T. Searle

Prof. Dr. Joshua T. Searle studied History at the University of Oxford and gained his PhD from Trinity College Dublin. He is Professor of Mission Studies and Intercultural Theology at the Theologische Hochschule Elstal near Berlin, and is also an ordained Pastor in the German Baptist Union. Previously, Searle was Director of Postgraduate Studies at Spurgeon's College, London. He is a Fellow of the Royal Historical Society and Fellow of the Higher Education Academy and serves as a founding Trustee of the UK-registered charity, Dnipro Hope Mission. His previous books include: *Theology After Christendom: Forming Prophets for a Post-Christian World* (2018), *A Future and a Hope: Mission, Theological Formation and the Transformation of Post-Soviet Society* (2014), *The Scarlet Woman and the Red Hand: Apocalyptic Belief in the Northern Ireland Troubles* (2014). His papers have been published by, among other outlets, "Oxford University Press", "Baylor University Press", "International Journal of Public Theology", and "European Journal of Theology".

Vladyslav Zaiets

Vladyslav Zaiets studied Law at the Kyiv University of Law of the National Academy of Sciences of Ukraine. Since 2022, he is a PhD Candidate in Civil Law at the Kyiv University of Law of the National Academy of Sciences of Ukraine. His previous works include Civil Law Limitations on Human Rights and Freedoms in Times of War and his articles such as Types of *Human Rights Limitations in the Context of Information Rights during Martial Law* (2024) and *Civil Law Protection of Personal Data in Martial Law Conditions: Ukrainian and International Experience* (2024). He is also a Research Fellow at the Institute of Religious Freedom. Zaiets is actively engaged in volunteer activities aimed at supporting human rights during times of conflict.

SOVIET AND POST-SOVIET POLITICS AND SOCIETY
Edited by Dr. Andreas Umland | ISSN 1614-3515

1. *Андреас Умланд (ред.)* | Воплощение Европейской конвенции по правам человека в России. Философские, юридические и эмпирические исследования | ISBN 3-89821-387-0

2. *Christian Wipperfürth* | Russland – ein vertrauenswürdiger Partner? Grundlagen, Hintergründe und Praxis gegenwärtiger russischer Außenpolitik | Mit einem Vorwort von Heinz Timmermann | ISBN 3-89821-401-X

3. *Manja Hussner* | Die Übernahme internationalen Rechts in die russische und deutsche Rechtsordnung. Eine vergleichende Analyse zur Völkerrechtsfreundlichkeit der Verfassungen der Russländischen Föderation und der Bundesrepublik Deutschland | Mit einem Vorwort von Rainer Arnold | ISBN 3-89821-438-9

4. *Matthew Tejada* | Bulgaria's Democratic Consolidation and the Kozloduy Nuclear Power Plant (KNPP). The Unattainability of Closure | With a foreword by Richard J. Crampton | ISBN 3-89821-439-7

5. *Марк Григорьевич Меерович* | Квадратные метры, определяющие сознание. Государственная жилищная политика в СССР. 1921 – 1941 гг | ISBN 3-89821-474-5

6. *Andrei P. Tsygankov, Pavel A. Tsygankov (Eds.)* | New Directions in Russian International Studies | ISBN 3-89821-422-2

7. *Марк Григорьевич Меерович* | Как власть народ к труду приучала. Жилище в СССР – средство управления людьми. 1917 – 1941 гг. | С предисловием Елены Осокиной | ISBN 3-89821-495-8

8. *David J. Galbreath* | Nation-Building and Minority Politics in Post-Socialist States. Interests, Influence and Identities in Estonia and Latvia | With a foreword by David J. Smith | ISBN 3-89821-467-2

9. *Алексей Юрьевич Безугольный* | Народы Кавказа в Вооруженных силах СССР в годы Великой Отечественной войны 1941-1945 гг. | С предисловием Николая Бугая | ISBN 3-89821-475-3

10. *Вячеслав Лихачев и Владимир Прибыловский (ред.)* | Русское Национальное Единство, 1990-2000. В 2-х томах | ISBN 3-89821-523-7

11. *Николай Бугай (ред.)* | Народы стран Балтии в условиях сталинизма (1940-е – 1950-е годы). Документированная история | ISBN 3-89821-525-3

12. *Ingmar Bredies (Hrsg.)* | Zur Anatomie der Orange Revolution in der Ukraine. Wechsel des Elitenregimes oder Triumph des Parlamentarismus? | ISBN 3-89821-524-5

13. *Anastasia V. Mitrofanova* | The Politicization of Russian Orthodoxy. Actors and Ideas | With a foreword by William C. Gay | ISBN 3-89821-481-8

14. *Nathan D. Larson* | Alexander Solzhenitsyn and the Russo-Jewish Question | ISBN 3-89821-483-4

15. *Guido Houben* | Kulturpolitik und Ethnizität. Staatliche Kunstförderung im Russland der neunziger Jahre | Mit einem Vorwort von Gert Weisskirchen | ISBN 3-89821-542-3

16. *Leonid Luks* | Der russische „Sonderweg"? Aufsätze zur neuesten Geschichte Russlands im europäischen Kontext | ISBN 3-89821-496-6

17. *Евгений Мороз* | История «Мёртвой воды» – от страшной сказки к большой политике. Политическое неоязычество в постсоветской России | ISBN 3-89821-551-2

18. *Александр Верховский и Галина Кожевникова (ред.)* | Этническая и религиозная интолерантность в российских СМИ. Результаты мониторинга 2001-2004 гг. | ISBN 3-89821-569-5

19. *Christian Ganzer* | Sowjetisches Erbe und ukrainische Nation. Das Museum der Geschichte des Zaporoger Kosakentums auf der Insel Chortycja | Mit einem Vorwort von Frank Golczewski | ISBN 3-89821-504-0

20. *Эльза-Баир Гучинова* | Помнить нельзя забыть. Антропология депортационной травмы калмыков | С предисловием Кэролайн Хамфри | ISBN 3-89821-506-7

21. *Юлия Лидерман* | Мотивы «проверки» и «испытания» в постсоветской культуре. Советское прошлое в российском кинематографе 1990-х годов | С предисловием Евгения Марголита | ISBN 3-89821-511-3

22. *Tanya Lokshina, Ray Thomas, Mary Mayer (Eds.)* | The Imposition of a Fake Political Settlement in the Northern Caucasus. The 2003 Chechen Presidential Election | ISBN 3-89821-436-2

23. *Timothy McCajor Hall, Rosie Read (Eds.)* | Changes in the Heart of Europe. Recent Ethnographies of Czechs, Slovaks, Roma, and Sorbs | With an afterword by Zdeněk Salzmann | ISBN 3-89821-606-5

24 *Christian Autengruber* | Die politischen Parteien in Bulgarien und Rumänien. Eine vergleichende Analyse seit Beginn der 90er Jahre | Mit einem Vorwort von Dorothée de Nève | ISBN 3-89821-476-1

25 *Annette Freyberg-Inan with Radu Cristescu* | The Ghosts in Our Classrooms, or: John Dewey Meets Ceauşescu. The Promise and the Failures of Civic Education in Romania | ISBN 3-89821-416-8

26 *John B. Dunlop* | The 2002 Dubrovka and 2004 Beslan Hostage Crises. A Critique of Russian Counter-Terrorism | With a foreword by Donald N. Jensen | ISBN 3-89821-608-X

27 *Peter Koller* | Das touristische Potenzial von Kam"janec'–Podil's'kyj. Eine fremdenverkehrsgeographische Untersuchung der Zukunftsperspektiven und Maßnahmenplanung zur Destinationsentwicklung des „ukrainischen Rothenburg" | Mit einem Vorwort von Kristiane Klemm | ISBN 3-89821-640-3

28 *Françoise Daucé, Elisabeth Sieca-Kozlowski (Eds.)* | Dedovshchina in the Post-Soviet Military. Hazing of Russian Army Conscripts in a Comparative Perspective | With a foreword by Dale Herspring | ISBN 3-89821-616-0

29 *Florian Strasser* | Zivilgesellschaftliche Einflüsse auf die Orange Revolution. Die gewaltlose Massenbewegung und die ukrainische Wahlkrise 2004 | Mit einem Vorwort von Egbert Jahn | ISBN 3-89821-648-9

30 *Rebecca S. Katz* | The Georgian Regime Crisis of 2003-2004. A Case Study in Post-Soviet Media Representation of Politics, Crime and Corruption | ISBN 3-89821-413-3

31 *Vladimir Kantor* | Willkür oder Freiheit. Beiträge zur russischen Geschichtsphilosophie | Ediert von Dagmar Herrmann sowie mit einem Vorwort versehen von Leonid Luks | ISBN 3-89821-589-X

32 *Laura A. Victoir* | The Russian Land Estate Today. A Case Study of Cultural Politics in Post-Soviet Russia | With a foreword by Priscilla Roosevelt | ISBN 3-89821-426-5

33 *Ivan Katchanovski* | Cleft Countries. Regional Political Divisions and Cultures in Post-Soviet Ukraine and Moldova | With a foreword by Francis Fukuyama | ISBN 3-89821-558-X

34 *Florian Mühlfried* | Postsowjetische Feiern. Das Georgische Bankett im Wandel | Mit einem Vorwort von Kevin Tuite | ISBN 3-89821-601-2

35 *Roger Griffin, Werner Loh, Andreas Umland (Eds.)* | Fascism Past and Present, West and East. An International Debate on Concepts and Cases in the Comparative Study of the Extreme Right | With an afterword by Walter Laqueur | ISBN 3-89821-674-8

36 *Sebastian Schlegel* | Der „Weiße Archipel". Sowjetische Atomstädte 1945-1991 | Mit einem Geleitwort von Thomas Bohn | ISBN 3-89821-679-9

37 *Vyacheslav Likhachev* | Political Anti-Semitism in Post-Soviet Russia. Actors and Ideas in 1991-2003 | Edited and translated from Russian by Eugene Veklerov | ISBN 3-89821-529-6

38 *Josette Baer (Ed.)* | Preparing Liberty in Central Europe. Political Texts from the Spring of Nations 1848 to the Spring of Prague 1968 | With a foreword by Zdeněk V. David | ISBN 3-89821-546-6

39 *Михаил Лукьянов* | Российский консерватизм и реформа, 1907-1914 | С предисловием Марка Д. Стейнберга | ISBN 3-89821-503-2

40 *Nicola Melloni* | Market Without Economy. The 1998 Russian Financial Crisis | With a foreword by Eiji Furukawa | ISBN 3-89821-407-9

41 *Dmitrij Chmelnizki* | Die Architektur Stalins | Bd. 1: Studien zu Ideologie und Stil | Bd. 2: Bilddokumentation | Mit einem Vorwort von Bruno Flierl | ISBN 3-89821-515-6

42 *Katja Yafimava* | Post-Soviet Russian-Belarussian Relationships. The Role of Gas Transit Pipelines | With a foreword by Jonathan P. Stern | ISBN 3-89821-655-1

43 *Boris Chavkin* | Verflechtungen der deutschen und russischen Zeitgeschichte. Aufsätze und Archivfunde zu den Beziehungen Deutschlands und der Sowjetunion von 1917 bis 1991 | Ediert von Markus Edlinger sowie mit einem Vorwort versehen von Leonid Luks | ISBN 3-89821-756-6

44 *Anastasija Grynenko in Zusammenarbeit mit Claudia Dathe* | Die Terminologie des Gerichtswesens der Ukraine und Deutschlands im Vergleich. Eine übersetzungswissenschaftliche Analyse juristischer Fachbegriffe im Deutschen, Ukrainischen und Russischen | Mit einem Vorwort von Ulrich Hartmann | ISBN 3-89821-691-8

45 *Anton Burkov* | The Impact of the European Convention on Human Rights on Russian Law. Legislation and Application in 1996-2006 | With a foreword by Françoise Hampson | ISBN 978-3-89821-639-5

46 *Stina Torjesen, Indra Overland (Eds.)* | International Election Observers in Post-Soviet Azerbaijan. Geopolitical Pawns or Agents of Change? | ISBN 978-3-89821-743-9

47 *Taras Kuzio* | Ukraine – Crimea – Russia. Triangle of Conflict | ISBN 978-3-89821-761-3

48 *Claudia Šabić* | „Ich erinnere mich nicht, aber L'viv!" Zur Funktion kultureller Faktoren für die Institutionalisierung und Entwicklung einer ukrainischen Region | Mit einem Vorwort von Melanie Tatur | ISBN 978-3-89821-752-1

49 Marlies Bilz | Tatarstan in der Transformation. Nationaler Diskurs und Politische Praxis 1988-1994 | Mit einem Vorwort von Frank Golczewski | ISBN 978-3-89821-722-4

50 Марлен Ларюэль (ред.) | Современные интерпретации русского национализма | ISBN 978-3-89821-795-8

51 Sonja Schüler | Die ethnische Dimension der Armut. Roma im postsozialistischen Rumänien | Mit einem Vorwort von Anton Sterbling | ISBN 978-3-89821-776-7

52 Галина Кожевникова | Радикальный национализм в России и противодействие ему. Сборник докладов Центра «Сова» за 2004-2007 гг. | С предисловием Александра Верховского | ISBN 978-3-89821-721-7

53 Галина Кожевникова и Владимир Прибыловский | Российская власть в биографиях I. Высшие должностные лица РФ в 2004 г. | ISBN 978-3-89821-796-5

54 Галина Кожевникова и Владимир Прибыловский | Российская власть в биографиях II. Члены Правительства РФ в 2004 г. | ISBN 978-3-89821-797-2

55 Галина Кожевникова и Владимир Прибыловский | Российская власть в биографиях III. Руководители федеральных служб и агентств РФ в 2004 г.| ISBN 978-3-89821-798-9

56 Ileana Petroniu | Privatisierung in Transformationsökonomien. Determinanten der Restrukturierungs-Bereitschaft am Beispiel Polens, Rumäniens und der Ukraine | Mit einem Vorwort von Rainer W. Schäfer | ISBN 978-3-89821-790-3

57 Christian Wipperfürth | Russland und seine GUS-Nachbarn. Hintergründe, aktuelle Entwicklungen und Konflikte in einer ressourcenreichen Region| ISBN 978-3-89821-801-6

58 Togzhan Kassenova | From Antagonism to Partnership. The Uneasy Path of the U.S.-Russian Cooperative Threat Reduction | With a foreword by Christoph Bluth | ISBN 978-3-89821-707-1

59 Alexander Höllwerth | Das sakrale eurasische Imperium des Aleksandr Dugin. Eine Diskursanalyse zum postsowjetischen russischen Rechtsextremismus | Mit einem Vorwort von Dirk Uffelmann | ISBN 978-3-89821-813-9

60 Олег Рябов | «Россия-Матушка». Национализм, гендер и война в России XX века | С предисловием Елены Гощило | ISBN 978-3-89821-487-2

61 Ivan Maistrenko | Borot'bism. A Chapter in the History of the Ukrainian Revolution | With a new Introduction by Chris Ford | Translated by George S. N. Luckyj with the assistance of Ivan L. Rudnytsky | Second, Revised and Expanded Edition ISBN 978-3-8382-1107-7

62 Maryna Romanets | Anamorphosic Texts and Reconfigured Visions. Improvised Traditions in Contemporary Ukrainian and Irish Literature | ISBN 978-3-89821-576-5

63 Paul D'Anieri and Taras Kuzio (Eds.) | Aspects of the Orange Revolution I. Democratization and Elections in Post-Communist Ukraine | ISBN 978-3-89821-698-2

64 Bohdan Harasymiw in collaboration with Oleh S. Ilnytzkyj (Eds.) | Aspects of the Orange Revolution II. Information and Manipulation Strategies in the 2004 Ukrainian Presidential Elections | ISBN 978-3-89821-699-9

65 Ingmar Bredies, Andreas Umland and Valentin Yakushik (Eds.) | Aspects of the Orange Revolution III. The Context and Dynamics of the 2004 Ukrainian Presidential Elections | ISBN 978-3-89821-803-0

66 Ingmar Bredies, Andreas Umland and Valentin Yakushik (Eds.) | Aspects of the Orange Revolution IV. Foreign Assistance and Civic Action in the 2004 Ukrainian Presidential Elections | ISBN 978-3-89821-808-5

67 Ingmar Bredies, Andreas Umland and Valentin Yakushik (Eds.) | Aspects of the Orange Revolution V. Institutional Observation Reports on the 2004 Ukrainian Presidential Elections | ISBN 978-3-89821-809-2

68 Taras Kuzio (Ed.) | Aspects of the Orange Revolution VI. Post-Communist Democratic Revolutions in Comparative Perspective | ISBN 978-3-89821-820-7

69 Tim Bohse | Autoritarismus statt Selbstverwaltung. Die Transformation der kommunalen Politik in der Stadt Kaliningrad 1990-2005 | Mit einem Geleitwort von Stefan Troebst | ISBN 978-3-89821-782-8

70 David Rupp | Die Rußländische Föderation und die russischsprachige Minderheit in Lettland. Eine Fallstudie zur Anwaltspolitik Moskaus gegenüber den russophonen Minderheiten im „Nahen Ausland" von 1991 bis 2002 | Mit einem Vorwort von Helmut Wagner | ISBN 978-3-89821-778-1

71 Taras Kuzio | Theoretical and Comparative Perspectives on Nationalism. New Directions in Cross-Cultural and Post-Communist Studies | With a foreword by Paul Robert Magocsi | ISBN 978-3-89821-815-3

72 Christine Teichmann | Die Hochschultransformation im heutigen Osteuropa. Kontinuität und Wandel bei der Entwicklung des postkommunistischen Universitätswesens | Mit einem Vorwort von Oskar Anweiler | ISBN 978-3-89821-842-8

73 *Julia Kusznir* | Der politische Einfluss von Wirtschaftseliten in russischen Regionen. Eine Analyse am Beispiel der Erdöl- und Erdgasindustrie, 1992-2005 | Mit einem Vorwort von Wolfgang Eichwede | ISBN 978-3-89821-821-4

74 *Alena Vysotskaya* | Russland, Belarus und die EU-Osterweiterung. Zur Minderheitenfrage und zum Problem der Freizügigkeit des Personenverkehrs | Mit einem Vorwort von Katlijn Malfliet | ISBN 978-3-89821-822-1

75 *Heiko Pleines (Hrsg.)* | Corporate Governance in post-sozialistischen Volkswirtschaften | ISBN 978-3-89821-766-8

76 *Stefan Ihrig* | Wer sind die Moldawier? Rumänismus versus Moldowanismus in Historiographie und Schulbüchern der Republik Moldova, 1991-2006 | Mit einem Vorwort von Holm Sundhaussen | ISBN 978-3-89821-466-7

77 *Galina Kozhevnikova in collaboration with Alexander Verkhovsky and Eugene Veklerov* | Ultra-Nationalism and Hate Crimes in Contemporary Russia. The 2004-2006 Annual Reports of Moscow's SOVA Center | With a foreword by Stephen D. Shenfield | ISBN 978-3-89821-868-9

78 *Florian Küchler* | The Role of the European Union in Moldova's Transnistria Conflict | With a foreword by Christopher Hill | ISBN 978-3-89821-850-4

79 *Bernd Rechel* | The Long Way Back to Europe. Minority Protection in Bulgaria | With a foreword by Richard Crampton | ISBN 978-3-89821-863-4

80 *Peter W. Rodgers* | Nation, Region and History in Post-Communist Transitions. Identity Politics in Ukraine, 1991-2006 | With a foreword by Vera Tolz | ISBN 978-3-89821-903-7

81 *Stephanie Solywoda* | The Life and Work of Semen L. Frank. A Study of Russian Religious Philosophy | With a foreword by Philip Walters | ISBN 978-3-89821-457-5

82 *Vera Sokolova* | Cultural Politics of Ethnicity. Discourses on Roma in Communist Czechoslovakia | ISBN 978-3-89821-864-1

83 *Natalya Shevchik Ketenci* | Kazakhstani Enterprises in Transition. The Role of Historical Regional Development in Kazakhstan's Post-Soviet Economic Transformation | ISBN 978-3-89821-831-3

84 *Martin Malek, Anna Schor-Tschudnowskaja (Hgg.)* | Europa im Tschetschenienkrieg. Zwischen politischer Ohnmacht und Gleichgültigkeit | Mit einem Vorwort von Lipchan Basajewa | ISBN 978-3-89821-676-0

85 *Stefan Meister* | Das postsowjetische Universitätswesen zwischen nationalem und internationalem Wandel. Die Entwicklung der regionalen Hochschule in Russland als Gradmesser der Systemtransformation | Mit einem Vorwort von Joan DeBardeleben | ISBN 978-3-89821-891-7

86 *Konstantin Sheiko in collaboration with Stephen Brown* | Nationalist Imaginings of the Russian Past. Anatolii Fomenko and the Rise of Alternative History in Post-Communist Russia | With a foreword by Donald Ostrowski | ISBN 978-3-89821-915-0

87 *Sabine Jenni* | Wie stark ist das „Einige Russland"? Zur Parteibindung der Eliten und zum Wahlerfolg der Machtpartei im Dezember 2007 | Mit einem Vorwort von Klaus Armingeon | ISBN 978-3-89821-961-7

88 *Thomas Borén* | Meeting-Places of Transformation. Urban Identity, Spatial Representations and Local Politics in Post-Soviet St Petersburg | ISBN 978-3-89821-739-2

89 *Aygul Ashirova* | Stalinismus und Stalin-Kult in Zentralasien. Turkmenistan 1924-1953 | Mit einem Vorwort von Leonid Luks | ISBN 978-3-89821-987-7

90 *Leonid Luks* | Freiheit oder imperiale Größe? Essays zu einem russischen Dilemma | ISBN 978-3-8382-0011-8

91 *Christopher Gilley* | The 'Change of Signposts' in the Ukrainian Emigration. A Contribution to the History of Sovietophilism in the 1920s | With a foreword by Frank Golczewski | ISBN 978-3-89821-965-5

92 *Philipp Casula, Jeronim Perovic (Eds.)* | Identities and Politics During the Putin Presidency. The Discursive Foundations of Russia's Stability | With a foreword by Heiko Haumann | ISBN 978-3-8382-0015-6

93 *Marcel Viëtor* | Europa und die Frage nach seinen Grenzen im Osten. Zur Konstruktion ‚europäischer Identität' in Geschichte und Gegenwart | Mit einem Vorwort von Albrecht Lehmann | ISBN 978-3-8382-0045-3

94 *Ben Hellman, Andrei Rogachevskii* | Filming the Unfilmable. Casper Wrede's 'One Day in the Life of Ivan Denisovich' | Second, Revised and Expanded Edition | ISBN 978-3-8382-0044-6

95 *Eva Fuchslocher* | Vaterland, Sprache, Glaube. Orthodoxie und Nationenbildung am Beispiel Georgiens | Mit einem Vorwort von Christina von Braun | ISBN 978-3-89821-884-9

96 *Vladimir Kantor* | Das Westlertum und der Weg Russlands. Zur Entwicklung der russischen Literatur und Philosophie | Ediert von Dagmar Herrmann | Mit einem Beitrag von Nikolaus Lobkowicz | ISBN 978-3-8382-0102-3

97 *Kamran Musayev* | Die postsowjetische Transformation im Baltikum und Südkaukasus. Eine vergleichende Untersuchung der politischen Entwicklung Lettlands und Aserbaidschans 1985-2009 | Mit einem Vorwort von Leonid Luks | Ediert von Sandro Henschel | ISBN 978-3-8382-0103-0

98 *Tatiana Zhurzhenko* | Borderlands into Bordered Lands. Geopolitics of Identity in Post-Soviet Ukraine | With a foreword by Dieter Segert | ISBN 978-3-8382-0042-2

99 *Кирилл Галушко, Лидия Смола (ред.)* | Пределы падения – варианты украинского будущего. Аналитико-прогностические исследования | ISBN 978-3-8382-0148-1

100 *Michael Minkenberg (Ed.)* | Historical Legacies and the Radical Right in Post-Cold War Central and Eastern Europe | With an afterword by Sabrina P. Ramet | ISBN 978-3-8382-0124-5

101 *David-Emil Wickström* | Rocking St. Petersburg. Transcultural Flows and Identity Politics in the St. Petersburg Popular Music Scene | With a foreword by Yngvar B. Steinholt | Second, Revised and Expanded Edition | ISBN 978-3-8382-0100-9

102 *Eva Zabka* | Eine neue „Zeit der Wirren"? Der spät- und postsowjetische Systemwandel 1985-2000 im Spiegel russischer gesellschaftspolitischer Diskurse | Mit einem Vorwort von Margareta Mommsen | ISBN 978-3-8382-0161-0

103 *Ulrike Ziemer* | Ethnic Belonging, Gender and Cultural Practices. Youth Identitites in Contemporary Russia | With a foreword by Anoop Nayak | ISBN 978-3-8382-0152-8

104 *Ksenia Chepikova* | ‚Einiges Russland' - eine zweite KPdSU? Aspekte der Identitätskonstruktion einer postsowjetischen „Partei der Macht" | Mit einem Vorwort von Torsten Oppelland | ISBN 978-3-8382-0311-9

105 *Леонид Люкс* | Западничество или евразийство? Демократия или идеократия? Сборник статей об исторических дилеммах России | С предисловием Владимира Кантора | ISBN 978-3-8382-0211-2

106 *Anna Dost* | Das russische Verfassungsrecht auf dem Weg zum Föderalismus und zurück. Zum Konflikt von Rechtsnormen und -wirklichkeit in der Russländischen Föderation von 1991 bis 2009 | Mit einem Vorwort von Alexander Blankenagel | ISBN 978-3-8382-0292-1

107 *Philipp Herzog* | Sozialistische Völkerfreundschaft, nationaler Widerstand oder harmloser Zeitvertreib? Zur politischen Funktion der Volkskunst im sowjetischen Estland | Mit einem Vorwort von Andreas Kappeler | ISBN 978-3-8382-0216-7

108 *Marlène Laruelle (Ed.)* | Russian Nationalism, Foreign Policy, and Identity Debates in Putin's Russia. New Ideological Patterns after the Orange Revolution | ISBN 978-3-8382-0325-6

109 *Michail Logvinov* | Russlands Kampf gegen den internationalen Terrorismus. Eine kritische Bestandsaufnahme des Bekämpfungsansatzes | Mit einem Geleitwort von Hans-Henning Schröder und einem Vorwort von Eckhard Jesse | ISBN 978-3-8382-0329-4

110 *John B. Dunlop* | The Moscow Bombings of September 1999. Examinations of Russian Terrorist Attacks at the Onset of Vladimir Putin's Rule | Second, Revised and Expanded Edition | ISBN 978-3-8382-0388-1

111 *Андрей А. Ковалёв* | Свидетельство из-за кулис российской политики I. Можно ли делать добро из зла? (Воспоминания и размышления о последних советских и первых послесоветских годах) | With a foreword by Peter Reddaway | ISBN 978-3-8382-0302-7

112 *Андрей А. Ковалёв* | Свидетельство из-за кулис российской политики II. Угроза для себя и окружающих (Наблюдения и предостережения относительно происходящего после 2000 г.) | ISBN 978-3-8382-0303-4

113 *Bernd Kappenberg* | Zeichen setzen für Europa. Der Gebrauch europäischer lateinischer Sonderzeichen in der deutschen Öffentlichkeit | Mit einem Vorwort von Peter Schlobinski | ISBN 978-3-89821-749-1

114 *Ivo Mijnssen* | The Quest for an Ideal Youth in Putin's Russia I. Back to Our Future! History, Modernity, and Patriotism according to Nashi, 2005-2013 | With a foreword by Jeronim Perović | Second, Revised and Expanded Edition | ISBN 978-3-8382-0368-3

115 *Jussi Lassila* | The Quest for an Ideal Youth in Putin's Russia II. The Search for Distinctive Conformism in the Political Communication of Nashi, 2005-2009 | With a foreword by Kirill Postoutenko | Second, Revised and Expanded Edition | ISBN 978-3-8382-0415-4

116 *Valerio Trabandt* | Neue Nachbarn, gute Nachbarschaft? Die EU als internationaler Akteur am Beispiel ihrer Demokratieförderung in Belarus und der Ukraine 2004-2009 | Mit einem Vorwort von Jutta Joachim | ISBN 978-3-8382-0437-6

117 *Fabian Pfeiffer* | Estlands Außen- und Sicherheitspolitik I. Der estnische Atlantizismus nach der wiedererlangten Unabhängigkeit 1991-2004 | Mit einem Vorwort von Helmut Hubel | ISBN 978-3-8382-0127-6

118 *Jana Podßuweit* | Estlands Außen- und Sicherheitspolitik II. Handlungsoptionen eines Kleinstaates im Rahmen seiner EU-Mitgliedschaft (2004-2008) | Mit einem Vorwort von Helmut Hubel | ISBN 978-3-8382-0440-6

119 *Karin Pointner* | Estlands Außen- und Sicherheitspolitik III. Eine gedächtnispolitische Analyse estnischer Entwicklungskooperation 2006-2010 | Mit einem Vorwort von Karin Liebhart | ISBN 978-3-8382-0435-2

120 *Ruslana Vovk* | Die Offenheit der ukrainischen Verfassung für das Völkerrecht und die europäische Integration | Mit einem Vorwort von Alexander Blankenagel | ISBN 978-3-8382-0481-9

121 *Mykhaylo Banakh* | Die Relevanz der Zivilgesellschaft bei den postkommunistischen Transformationsprozessen in mittel- und osteuropäischen Ländern. Das Beispiel der spät- und postsowjetischen Ukraine 1986-2009 | Mit einem Vorwort von Gerhard Simon | ISBN 978-3-8382-0499-4

122 *Michael Moser* | Language Policy and the Discourse on Languages in Ukraine under President Viktor Yanukovych (25 February 2010–28 October 2012) | ISBN 978-3-8382-0497-0 (Paperback edition) | ISBN 978-3-8382-0507-6 (Hardcover edition)

123 *Nicole Krome* | Russischer Netzwerkkapitalismus Restrukturierungsprozesse in der Russischen Föderation am Beispiel des Luftfahrtunternehmens „Aviastar" | Mit einem Vorwort von Petra Stykow | ISBN 978-3-8382-0534-2

124 *David R. Marples* | 'Our Glorious Past'. Lukashenka's Belarus and the Great Patriotic War | ISBN 978-3-8382-0574-8 (Paperback edition) | ISBN 978-3-8382-0675-2 (Hardcover edition)

125 *Ulf Walther* | Russlands „neuer Adel". Die Macht des Geheimdienstes von Gorbatschow bis Putin | Mit einem Vorwort von Hans-Georg Wieck | ISBN 978-3-8382-0584-7

126 *Simon Geissbühler (Hrsg.)* | Kiew – Revolution 3.0. Der Euromaidan 2013/14 und die Zukunftsperspektiven der Ukraine | ISBN 978-3-8382-0581-6 (Paperback edition) | ISBN 978-3-8382-0681-3 (Hardcover edition)

127 *Andrey Makarychev* | Russia and the EU in a Multipolar World. Discourses, Identities, Norms | With a foreword by Klaus Segbers | ISBN 978-3-8382-0629-5

128 *Roland Scharff* | Kasachstan als postsowjetischer Wohlfahrtsstaat. Die Transformation des sozialen Schutzsystems | Mit einem Vorwort von Joachim Ahrens | ISBN 978-3-8382-0622-6

129 *Katja Grupp* | Bild Lücke Deutschland. Kaliningrader Studierende sprechen über Deutschland | Mit einem Vorwort von Martin Schulz | ISBN 978-3-8382-0552-6

130 *Konstantin Sheiko, Stephen Brown* | History as Therapy. Alternative History and Nationalist Imaginings in Russia, 1991-2014 | ISBN 978-3-8382-0665-3

131 *Elisa Kriza* | Alexander Solzhenitsyn: Cold War Icon, Gulag Author, Russian Nationalist? A Study of the Western Reception of his Literary Writings, Historical Interpretations, and Political Ideas | With a foreword by Andrei Rogatchevski | ISBN 978-3-8382-0589-2 (Paperback edition) | ISBN 978-3-8382-0690-5 (Hardcover edition)

132 *Serghei Golunov* | The Elephant in the Room. Corruption and Cheating in Russian Universities | ISBN 978-3-8382-0570-0

133 *Manja Hussner, Rainer Arnold (Hgg.)* | Verfassungsgerichtsbarkeit in Zentralasien I. Sammlung von Verfassungstexten | ISBN 978-3-8382-0595-3

134 *Nikolay Mitrokhin* | Die „Russische Partei". Die Bewegung der russischen Nationalisten in der UdSSR 1953-1985 | Aus dem Russischen übertragen von einem Übersetzerteam unter der Leitung von Larisa Schippel | ISBN 978-3-8382-0024-8

135 *Manja Hussner, Rainer Arnold (Hgg.)* | Verfassungsgerichtsbarkeit in Zentralasien II. Sammlung von Verfassungstexten | ISBN 978-3-8382-0597-7

136 *Manfred Zeller* | Das sowjetische Fieber. Fußballfans im poststalinistischen Vielvölkerreich | Mit einem Vorwort von Nikolaus Katzer | ISBN 978-3-8382-0757-5

137 *Kristin Schreiter* | Stellung und Entwicklungspotential zivilgesellschaftlicher Gruppen in Russland. Menschenrechtsorganisationen im Vergleich | ISBN 978-3-8382-0673-8

138 *David R. Marples, Frederick V. Mills (Eds.)* | Ukraine's Euromaidan. Analyses of a Civil Revolution | ISBN 978-3-8382-0660-8

139 *Bernd Kappenberg* | Setting Signs for Europe. Why Diacritics Matter for European Integration | With a foreword by Peter Schlobinski | ISBN 978-3-8382-0663-9

140 *René Lenz* | Internationalisierung, Kooperation und Transfer. Externe bildungspolitische Akteure in der Russischen Föderation | Mit einem Vorwort von Frank Ettrich | ISBN 978-3-8382-0751-3

141 *Juri Plusnin, Yana Zausaeva, Natalia Zhidkevich, Artemy Pozanenko* | Wandering Workers. Mores, Behavior, Way of Life, and Political Status of Domestic Russian Labor Migrants | Translated by Julia Kazantseva | ISBN 978-3-8382-0653-0

142 *David J. Smith (Eds.)* | Latvia – A Work in Progress? 100 Years of State- and Nation-Building | ISBN 978-3-8382-0648-6

143 *Инна Чувычкина (ред.)* | Экспортные нефте- и газопроводы на постсоветском пространстве. Анализ трубопроводной политики в свете теории международных отношений | ISBN 978-3-8382-0822-0

144　*Johann Zajaczkowski* | Russland – eine pragmatische Großmacht? Eine rollentheoretische Untersuchung russischer Außenpolitik am Beispiel der Zusammenarbeit mit den USA nach 9/11 und des Georgienkrieges von 2008 | Mit einem Vorwort von Siegfried Schieder | ISBN 978-3-8382-0837-4

145　*Boris Popivanov* | Changing Images of the Left in Bulgaria. The Challenge of Post-Communism in the Early 21st Century | ISBN 978-3-8382-0667-7

146　*Lenka Krátká* | A History of the Czechoslovak Ocean Shipping Company 1948-1989. How a Small, Landlocked Country Ran Maritime Business During the Cold War | ISBN 978-3-8382-0666-0

147　*Alexander Sergunin* | Explaining Russian Foreign Policy Behavior. Theory and Practice | ISBN 978-3-8382-0752-0

148　*Darya Malyutina* | Migrant Friendships in a Super-Diverse City. Russian-Speakers and their Social Relationships in London in the 21st Century | With a foreword by Claire Dwyer | ISBN 978-3-8382-0652-3

149　*Alexander Sergunin, Valery Konyshev* | Russia in the Arctic. Hard or Soft Power? | ISBN 978-3-8382-0753-7

150　*John J. Maresca* | Helsinki Revisited. A Key U.S. Negotiator's Memoirs on the Development of the CSCE into the OSCE | With a foreword by Hafiz Pashayev | ISBN 978-3-8382-0852-7

151　*Jardar Østbø* | The New Third Rome. Readings of a Russian Nationalist Myth | With a foreword by Pål Kolstø | ISBN 978-3-8382-0870-1

152　*Simon Kordonsky* | Socio-Economic Foundations of the Russian Post-Soviet Regime. The Resource-Based Economy and Estate-Based Social Structure of Contemporary Russia | With a foreword by Svetlana Barsukova | ISBN 978-3-8382-0775-9

153　*Duncan Leitch* | Assisting Reform in Post-Communist Ukraine 2000–2012. The Illusions of Donors and the Disillusion of Beneficiaries | With a foreword by Kataryna Wolczuk | ISBN 978-3-8382-0844-2

154　*Abel Polese* | Limits of a Post-Soviet State. How Informality Replaces, Renegotiates, and Reshapes Governance in Contemporary Ukraine | With a foreword by Colin Williams | ISBN 978-3-8382-0845-9

155　*Mikhail Suslov (Ed.)* | Digital Orthodoxy in the Post-Soviet World. The Russian Orthodox Church and Web 2.0 | With a foreword by Father Cyril Hovorun | ISBN 978-3-8382-0871-8

156　*Leonid Luks* | Zwei „Sonderwege"? Russisch-deutsche Parallelen und Kontraste (1917-2014). Vergleichende Essays | ISBN 978-3-8382-0823-7

157　*Vladimir V. Karacharovskiy, Ovsey I. Shkaratan, Gordey A. Yastrebov* | Towards a New Russian Work Culture. Can Western Companies and Expatriates Change Russian Society? | With a foreword by Elena N. Danilova | Translated by Julia Kazantseva | ISBN 978-3-8382-0902-9

158　*Edmund Griffiths* | Aleksandr Prokhanov and Post-Soviet Esotericism | ISBN 978-3-8382-0963-0

159　*Timm Beichelt, Susann Worschech (Eds.)* | Transnational Ukraine? Networks and Ties that Influence(d) Contemporary Ukraine | ISBN 978-3-8382-0944-9

160　*Mieste Hotopp-Riecke* | Die Tataren der Krim zwischen Assimilation und Selbstbehauptung. Der Aufbau des krimtatarischen Bildungswesens nach Deportation und Heimkehr (1990-2005) | Mit einem Vorwort von Swetlana Czerwonnaja | ISBN 3-89821-940-2

161　*Olga Bertelsen (Ed.)* | Revolution and War in Contemporary Ukraine. The Challenge of Change | ISBN 978-3-8382-1016-2

162　*Natalya Ryabinska* | Ukraine's Post-Communist Mass Media. Between Capture and Commercialization | With a foreword by Marta Dyczok | ISBN 978-3-8382-1011-7

163　*Alexandra Cotofana, James M. Nyce (Eds.)* | Religion and Magic in Socialist and Post-Socialist Contexts. Historic and Ethnographic Case Studies of Orthodoxy, Heterodoxy, and Alternative Spirituality | With a foreword by Patrick L. Michelson | ISBN 978-3-8382-0989-0

164　*Nozima Akhrarkhodjaeva* | The Instrumentalisation of Mass Media in Electoral Authoritarian Regimes. Evidence from Russia's Presidential Election Campaigns of 2000 and 2008 | ISBN 978-3-8382-1013-1

165　*Yulia Krasheninnikova* | Informal Healthcare in Contemporary Russia. Sociographic Essays on the Post-Soviet Infrastructure for Alternative Healing Practices | ISBN 978-3-8382-0970-8

166　*Peter Kaiser* | Das Schachbrett der Macht. Die Handlungsspielräume eines sowjetischen Funktionärs unter Stalin am Beispiel des Generalsekretärs des Komsomol Aleksandr Kosarev (1929-1938) | Mit einem Vorwort von Dietmar Neutatz | ISBN 978-3-8382-1052-0

167　*Oksana Kim* | The Effects and Implications of Kazakhstan's Adoption of International Financial Reporting Standards. A Resource Dependence Perspective | With a foreword by Svetlana Vlady | ISBN 978-3-8382-0987-6

168 *Anna Sanina* | Patriotic Education in Contemporary Russia. Sociological Studies in the Making of the Post-Soviet Citizen | With a foreword by Anna Oldfield | ISBN 978-3-8382-0993-7

169 *Rudolf Wolters* | Spezialist in Sibirien Faksimile der 1933 erschienenen ersten Ausgabe | Mit einem Vorwort von Dmitrij Chmelnizki | ISBN 978-3-8382-0515-1

170 *Michal Vít, Magdalena M. Baran (Eds.)* | Transregional versus National Perspectives on Contemporary Central European History. Studies on the Building of Nation-States and Their Cooperation in the 20th and 21st Century | With a foreword by Petr Vágner | ISBN 978-3-8382-1015-5

171 *Philip Gamaghelyan* | Conflict Resolution Beyond the International Relations Paradigm. Evolving Designs as a Transformative Practice in Nagorno-Karabakh and Syria | With a foreword by Susan Allen | ISBN 978-3-8382-1057-5

172 *Maria Shagina* | Joining a Prestigious Club. Cooperation with Europarties and Its Impact on Party Development in Georgia, Moldova, and Ukraine 2004–2015 | With a foreword by Kataryna Wolczuk | ISBN 978-3-8382-1084-1

173 *Alexandra Cotofana, James M. Nyce (Eds.)* | Religion and Magic in Socialist and Post-Socialist Contexts II. Baltic, Eastern European, and Post-USSR Case Studies | With a foreword by Anita Stasulane | ISBN 978-3-8382-0990-6

174 *Barbara Kunz* | Kind Words, Cruise Missiles, and Everything in Between. The Use of Power Resources in U.S. Policies towards Poland, Ukraine, and Belarus 1989–2008 | With a foreword by William Hill | ISBN 978-3-8382-1065-0

175 *Eduard Klein* | Bildungskorruption in Russland und der Ukraine. Eine komparative Analyse der Performanz staatlicher Antikorruptionsmaßnahmen im Hochschulsektor am Beispiel universitärer Aufnahmeprüfungen | Mit einem Vorwort von Heiko Pleines | ISBN 978-3-8382-0995-1

176 *Markus Soldner* | Politischer Kapitalismus im postsowjetischen Russland. Die politische, wirtschaftliche und mediale Transformation in den 1990er Jahren | Mit einem Vorwort von Wolfgang Ismayr | ISBN 978-3-8382-1222-7

177 *Anton Oleinik* | Building Ukraine from Within. A Sociological, Institutional, and Economic Analysis of a Nation-State in the Making | ISBN 978-3-8382-1150-3

178 *Peter Rollberg, Marlene Laruelle (Eds.)* | Mass Media in the Post-Soviet World. Market Forces, State Actors, and Political Manipulation in the Informational Environment after Communism | ISBN 978-3-8382-1116-9

179 *Mikhail Minakov* | Development and Dystopia. Studies in Post-Soviet Ukraine and Eastern Europe | With a foreword by Alexander Etkind | ISBN 978-3-8382-1112-1

180 *Aijan Sharshenova* | The European Union's Democracy Promotion in Central Asia. A Study of Political Interests, Influence, and Development in Kazakhstan and Kyrgyzstan in 2007–2013 | With a foreword by Gordon Crawford | ISBN 978-3-8382-1151-0

181 *Andrey Makarychev, Alexandra Yatsyk (Eds.)* | Boris Nemtsov and Russian Politics. Power and Resistance | With a foreword by Zhanna Nemtsova | ISBN 978-3-8382-1122-0

182 *Sophie Falsini* | The Euromaidan's Effect on Civil Society. Why and How Ukrainian Social Capital Increased after the Revolution of Dignity | With a foreword by Susann Worschech | ISBN 978-3-8382-1131-2

183 *Valentyna Romanova, Andreas Umland (Eds.)* | Ukraine's Decentralization. Challenges and Implications of the Local Governance Reform after the Euromaidan Revolution | ISBN 978-3-8382-1162-6

184 *Leonid Luks* | A Fateful Triangle. Essays on Contemporary Russian, German and Polish History | ISBN 978-3-8382-1143-5

185 *John B. Dunlop* | The February 2015 Assassination of Boris Nemtsov and the Flawed Trial of his Alleged Killers. An Exploration of Russia's "Crime of the 21st Century" | ISBN 978-3-8382-1188-6

186 *Vasile Rotaru* | Russia, the EU, and the Eastern Partnership. Building Bridges or Digging Trenches? | ISBN 978-3-8382-1134-3

187 *Marina Lebedeva* | Russian Studies of International Relations. From the Soviet Past to the Post-Cold-War Present | With a foreword by Andrei P. Tsygankov | ISBN 978-3-8382-0851-0

188 *Tomasz Stępniewski, George Soroka (Eds.)* | Ukraine after Maidan. Revisiting Domestic and Regional Security | ISBN 978-3-8382-1075-9

189 *Petar Cholakov* | Ethnic Entrepreneurs Unmasked. Political Institutions and Ethnic Conflicts in Contemporary Bulgaria | ISBN 978-3-8382-1189-3

190 *A. Salem, G. Hazeldine, D. Morgan (Eds.)* | Higher Education in Post-Communist States. Comparative and Sociological Perspectives | ISBN 978-3-8382-1183-1

191 *Igor Torbakov* | After Empire. Nationalist Imagination and Symbolic Politics in Russia and Eurasia in the Twentieth and Twenty-First Century | With a foreword by Serhii Plokhy | ISBN 978-3-8382-1217-3

192 *Aleksandr Burakovskiy* | Jewish-Ukrainian Relations in Late and Post-Soviet Ukraine. Articles, Lectures and Essays from 1986 to 2016 | ISBN 978-3-8382-1210-4

193 *Natalia Shapovalova, Olga Burlyuk (Eds.)* | Civil Society in Post-Euromaidan Ukraine. From Revolution to Consolidation | With a foreword by Richard Youngs | ISBN 978-3-8382-1216-6

194 *Franz Preissler* | Positionsverteidigung, Imperialismus oder Irredentismus? Russland und die „Russischsprachigen", 1991–2015 | ISBN 978-3-8382-1262-3

195 *Marian Madeła* | Der Reformprozess in der Ukraine 2014-2017. Eine Fallstudie zur Reform der öffentlichen Verwaltung | Mit einem Vorwort von Martin Malek | ISBN 978-3-8382-1266-1

196 *Anke Giesen* | „Wie kann denn der Sieger ein Verbrecher sein?" Eine diskursanalytische Untersuchung der russlandweiten Debatte über Konzept und Verstaatlichungsprozess der Lagergedenkstätte „Perm'-36" im Ural | ISBN 978-3-8382-1284-5

197 *Victoria Leukavets* | The Integration Policies of Belarus and Ukraine vis-à-vis the EU and Russia. A Comparative Analysis Through the Prism of a Two-Level Game Approach | ISBN 978-3-8382-1247-0

198 *Oksana Kim* | The Development and Challenges of Russian Corporate Governance I. The Roles and Functions of Boards of Directors | With a foreword by Sheila M. Puffer | ISBN 978-3-8382-1287-6

199 *Thomas D. Grant* | International Law and the Post-Soviet Space I. Essays on Chechnya and the Baltic States | With a foreword by Stephen M. Schwebel | ISBN 978-3-8382-1279-1

200 *Thomas D. Grant* | International Law and the Post-Soviet Space II. Essays on Ukraine, Intervention, and Non-Proliferation | ISBN 978-3-8382-1280-7

201 *Slavomír Michálek, Michal Štefansky* | The Age of Fear. The Cold War and Its Influence on Czechoslovakia 1945–1968 | ISBN 978-3-8382-1285-2

202 *Iulia-Sabina Joja* | Romania's Strategic Culture 1990–2014. Continuity and Change in a Post-Communist Country's Evolution of National Interests and Security Policies | With a foreword by Heiko Biehl | ISBN 978-3-8382-1286-9

203 *Andrei Rogatchevski, Yngvar B. Steinholt, Arve Hansen, David-Emil Wickström* | War of Songs. Popular Music and Recent Russia-Ukraine Relations | With a foreword by Artemy Troitsky | ISBN 978-3-8382-1173-2

204 *Maria Lipman (Ed.)* | Russian Voices on Post-Crimea Russia. An Almanac of Counterpoint Essays from 2015–2018 | ISBN 978-3-8382-1251-7

205 *Ksenia Maksimovtsova* | Language Conflicts in Contemporary Estonia, Latvia, and Ukraine. A Comparative Exploration of Discourses in Post-Soviet Russian-Language Digital Media | With a foreword by Ammon Cheskin | ISBN 978-3-8382-1282-1

206 *Michal Vit* | The EU's Impact on Identity Formation in East-Central Europe between 2004 and 2013. Perceptions of the Nation and Europe in Political Parties of the Czech Republic, Poland, and Slovakia | With a foreword by Andrea Pető | ISBN 978-3-8382-1275-3

207 *Per A. Rudling* | Tarnished Heroes. The Organization of Ukrainian Nationalists in the Memory Politics of Post-Soviet Ukraine | ISBN 978-3-8382-0999-9

208 *Kaja Gadowska, Peter Solomon (Eds.)* | Legal Change in Post-Communist States. Progress, Reversions, Explanations | ISBN 978-3-8382-1312-5

209 *Paweł Kowal, Georges Mink, Iwona Reichardt (Eds.)* | Three Revolutions: Mobilization and Change in Contemporary Ukraine I. Theoretical Aspects and Analyses on Religion, Memory, and Identity | ISBN 978-3-8382-1321-7

210 *Paweł Kowal, Georges Mink, Adam Reichardt, Iwona Reichardt (Eds.)* | Three Revolutions: Mobilization and Change in Contemporary Ukraine II. An Oral History of the Revolution on Granite, Orange Revolution, and Revolution of Dignity | ISBN 978-3-8382-1323-1

211 *Li Bennich-Björkman, Sergiy Kurbatov (Eds.)* | When the Future Came. The Collapse of the USSR and the Emergence of National Memory in Post-Soviet History Textbooks | ISBN 978-3-8382-1335-4

212 *Olga R. Gulina* | Migration as a (Geo-)Political Challenge in the Post-Soviet Space. Border Regimes, Policy Choices, Visa Agendas | With a foreword by Nils Muižnieks | ISBN 978-3-8382-1338-5

213 *Sanna Turoma, Kaarina Aitamurto, Slobodanka Vladiv-Glover (Eds.)* | Religion, Expression, and Patriotism in Russia. Essays on Post-Soviet Society and the State. ISBN 978-3-8382-1346-0

214 *Vasif Huseynov* | Geopolitical Rivalries in the "Common Neighborhood". Russia's Conflict with the West, Soft Power, and Neoclassical Realism | With a foreword by Nicholas Ross Smith | ISBN 978-3-8382-1277-7

215 *Mikhail Suslov* | Geopolitical Imagination. Ideology and Utopia in Post-Soviet Russia | With a foreword by Mark Bassin | ISBN 978-3-8382-1361-3

216 *Alexander Etkind, Mikhail Minakov (Eds.)* | Ideology after Union. Political Doctrines, Discourses, and Debates in Post-Soviet Societies | ISBN 978-3-8382-1388-0

217 *Jakob Mischke, Oleksandr Zabirko (Hgg.)* | Protestbewegungen im langen Schatten des Kreml. Aufbruch und Resignation in Russland und der Ukraine | ISBN 978-3-8382-0926-5

218 *Oksana Huss* | How Corruption and Anti-Corruption Policies Sustain Hybrid Regimes. Strategies of Political Domination under Ukraine's Presidents in 1994-2014 | With a foreword by Tobias Debiel and Andrea Gawrich | ISBN 978-3-8382-1430-6

219 *Dmitry Travin, Vladimir Gel'man, Otar Marganiya* | The Russian Path. Ideas, Interests, Institutions, Illusions | With a foreword by Vladimir Ryzhkov | ISBN 978-3-8382-1421-4

220 *Gergana Dimova* | Political Uncertainty. A Comparative Exploration | With a foreword by Todor Yalamov and Rumena Filipova | ISBN 978-3-8382-1385-9

221 *Torben Waschke* | Russland in Transition. Geopolitik zwischen Raum, Identität und Machtinteressen | Mit einem Vorwort von Andreas Dittmann | ISBN 978-3-8382-1480-1

222 *Steven Jobbitt, Zsolt Bottlik, Marton Berki (Eds.)* | Power and Identity in the Post-Soviet Realm. Geographies of Ethnicity and Nationality after 1991 | ISBN 978-3-8382-1399-6

223 *Daria Buteiko* | Erinnerungsort. Ort des Gedenkens, der Erholung oder der Einkehr? Kommunismus-Erinnerung am Beispiel der Gedenkstätte Berliner Mauer sowie des Soloveckij-Klosters und -Museumsparks | ISBN 978-3-8382-1367-5

224 *Olga Bertelsen (Ed.)* | Russian Active Measures. Yesterday, Today, Tomorrow | With a foreword by Jan Goldman | ISBN 978-3-8382-1529-7

225 *David Mandel* | "Optimizing" Higher Education in Russia. University Teachers and their Union "Universitetskaya solidarnost'" | ISBN 978-3-8382-1519-8

226 *Mikhail Minakov, Gwendolyn Sasse, Daria Isachenko (Eds.)* | Post-Soviet Secessionism. Nation-Building and State-Failure after Communism | ISBN 978-3-8382-1538-9

227 *Jakob Hauter (Ed.)* | Civil War? Interstate War? Hybrid War? Dimensions and Interpretations of the Donbas Conflict in 2014–2020 | With a foreword by Andrew Wilson | ISBN 978-3-8382-1383-5

228 *Tima T. Moldogaziev, Gene A. Brewer, J. Edward Kellough (Eds.)* | Public Policy and Politics in Georgia. Lessons from Post-Soviet Transition | With a foreword by Dan Durning | ISBN 978-3-8382-1535-8

229 *Oxana Schmies (Ed.)* | NATO's Enlargement and Russia. A Strategic Challenge in the Past and Future | With a foreword by Vladimir Kara-Murza | ISBN 978-3-8382-1478-8

230 *Christopher Ford* | Ukapisme – Une Gauche perdue. Le marxisme anti-colonial dans la révolution ukrainienne 1917-1925 | Avec une préface de Vincent Présumey | ISBN 978-3-8382-0899-2

231 *Anna Kutkina* | Between Lenin and Bandera. Decommunization and Multivocality in Post-Euromaidan Ukraine | With a foreword by Juri Mykkänen | ISBN 978-3-8382-1506-8

232 *Lincoln E. Flake* | Defending the Faith. The Russian Orthodox Church and the Demise of Religious Pluralism | With a foreword by Peter Martland | ISBN 978-3-8382-1378-1

233 *Nikoloz Samkharadze* | Russia's Recognition of the Independence of Abkhazia and South Ossetia. Analysis of a Deviant Case in Moscow's Foreign Policy | With a foreword by Neil MacFarlane | ISBN 978-3-8382-1414-6

234 *Arve Hansen* | Urban Protest. A Spatial Perspective on Kyiv, Minsk, and Moscow | With a foreword by Julie Wilhelmsen | ISBN 978-3-8382-1495-5

235 *Eleonora Narvselius, Julie Fedor (Eds.)* | Diversity in the East-Central European Borderlands. Memories, Cityscapes, People | ISBN 978-3-8382-1523-5

236 *Regina Elsner* | The Russian Orthodox Church and Modernity. A Historical and Theological Investigation into Eastern Christianity between Unity and Plurality | With a foreword by Mikhail Suslov | ISBN 978-3-8382-1568-6

237 *Bo Petersson* | The Putin Predicament. Problems of Legitimacy and Succession in Russia | With a foreword by J. Paul Goode | ISBN 978-3-8382-1050-6

238 *Jonathan Otto Pohl* | The Years of Great Silence. The Deportation, Special Settlement, and Mobilization into the Labor Army of Ethnic Germans in the USSR, 1941–1955 | ISBN 978-3-8382-1630-0

239 *Mikhail Minakov (Ed.)* | Inventing Majorities. Ideological Creativity in Post-Soviet Societies | ISBN 978-3-8382-1641-6

240 *Robert M. Cutler* | Soviet and Post-Soviet Foreign Policies I. East-South Relations and the Political Economy of the Communist Bloc, 1971–1991 | With a foreword by Roger E. Kanet | ISBN 978-3-8382-1654-5

241 *Izabella Agardi* | On the Verge of History. Life Stories of Rural Women from Serbia, Romania, and Hungary, 1920–2020 | With a foreword by Andrea Pető | ISBN 978-3-8382-1602-7

242 *Sebastian Schäffer (Ed.)* | Ukraine in Central and Eastern Europe. Kyiv's Foreign Affairs and the International Relations of the Post-Communist Region | With a foreword by Pavlo Klimkin and Andreas Umland| ISBN 978-3-8382-1615-7

243 *Volodymyr Dubrovskyi, Kalman Mizsei, Mychailo Wynnyckyj (Eds.)* | Eight Years after the Revolution of Dignity. What Has Changed in Ukraine during 2013–2021? | With a foreword by Yaroslav Hrytsak | ISBN 978-3-8382-1560-0

244 *Rumena Filipova* | Constructing the Limits of Europe Identity and Foreign Policy in Poland, Bulgaria, and Russia since 1989 | With forewords by Harald Wydra and Gergana Yankova-Dimova | ISBN 978-3-8382-1649-2

245 *Oleksandra Keudel* | How Patronal Networks Shape Opportunities for Local Citizen Participation in a Hybrid Regime A Comparative Analysis of Five Cities in Ukraine | With a foreword by Sabine Kropp | ISBN 978-3-8382-1671-3

246 *Jan Claas Behrends, Thomas Lindenberger, Pavel Kolar (Eds.)* | Violence after Stalin Institutions, Practices, and Everyday Life in the Soviet Bloc 1953–1989 | ISBN 978-3-8382-1637-9

247 *Leonid Luks* | Macht und Ohnmacht der Utopien Essays zur Geschichte Russlands im 20. und 21. Jahrhundert | ISBN 978-3-8382-1677-5

248 *Iuliia Barshadska* | Brüssel zwischen Kyjiw und Moskau Das auswärtige Handeln der Europäischen Union im ukrainisch-russischen Konflikt 2014-2019 | Mit einem Vorwort von Olaf Leiße | ISBN 978-3-8382-1667-6

249 *Valentyna Romanova* | Decentralisation and Multilevel Elections in Ukraine Reform Dynamics and Party Politics in 2010–2021 | With a foreword by Kimitaka Matsuzato | ISBN 978-3-8382-1700-0

250 *Alexander Motyl* | National Questions. Theoretical Reflections on Nations and Nationalism in Eastern Europe | ISBN 978-3-8382-1675-1

251 *Marc Dietrich* | A Cosmopolitan Model for Peacebuilding. The Ukrainian Cases of Crimea and the Donbas | With a foreword by Rémi Baudouï | ISBN 978-3-8382-1687-4

252 *Eduard Baidaus* | An Unsettled Nation. Moldova in the Geopolitics of Russia, Romania, and Ukraine | With forewords by John-Paul Himka and David R. Marples | ISBN 978-3-8382-1582-2

253 *Igor Okunev, Petr Oskolkov (Eds.)* | Transforming the Administrative Matryoshka. The Reform of Autonomous Okrugs in the Russian Federation, 2003–2008 | With a foreword by Vladimir Zorin | ISBN 978-3-8382-1721-5

254 *Winfried Schneider-Deters* | Ukraine's Fateful Years 2013–2019. Vol. I: The Popular Uprising in Winter 2013/2014 | ISBN 978-3-8382-1725-3

255 *Winfried Schneider-Deters* | Ukraine's Fateful Years 2013–2019. Vol. II: The Annexation of Crimea and the War in Donbas | ISBN 978-3-8382-1726-0

256 *Robert M. Cutler* | Soviet and Post-Soviet Russian Foreign Policies II. East-West Relations in Europe and the Political Economy of the Communist Bloc, 1971–1991 | With a foreword by Roger E. Kanet | ISBN 978-3-8382-1727-7

257 *Robert M. Cutler* | Soviet and Post-Soviet Russian Foreign Policies III. East-West Relations in Europe and Eurasia in the Post-Cold War Transition, 1991–2001 | With a foreword by Roger E. Kanet | ISBN 978-3-8382-1728-4

258 *Paweł Kowal, Iwona Reichardt, Kateryna Pryshchepa (Eds.)* | Three Revolutions: Mobilization and Change in Contemporary Ukraine III. Archival Records and Historical Sources on the 1990 Revolution on Granite | ISBN 978-3-8382-1376-7

259 *Mikhail Minakov (Ed.)* | Philosophy Unchained. Developments in Post-Soviet Philosophical Thought. | With a foreword by Christopher Donohue | ISBN 978-3-8382-1768-0

260 *David Dalton* | The Ukrainian Oligarchy After the Euromaidan. How Ukraine's Political Economy Regime Survived the Crisis | With a foreword by Andrew Wilson | ISBN 978-3-8382-1740-6

261 *Andreas Heinemann-Grüder (Ed.)* | Who Are the Fighters? Irregular Armed Groups in the Russian-Ukrainian War since 2014 | ISBN 978-3-8382-1777-2

262 *Taras Kuzio (Ed.)* | Russian Disinformation and Western Scholarship. Bias and Prejudice in Journalistic, Expert, and Academic Analyses of East European, Russian and Eurasian Affairs | ISBN 978-3-8382-1685-0

263 *Darius Furmonavicius* | LithuaniaTransforms the West. Lithuania's Liberation from Soviet Occupation and the Enlargement of NATO (1988–2022) | With a foreword by Vytautas Landsbergis | ISBN 978-3-8382-1779-6

264 *Dirk Dalberg* | Politisches Denken im tschechoslowakischen Dissens. Egon Bondy, Miroslav Kusý, Milan Šimečka und Petr Uhl (1968-1989) | ISBN 978-3-8382-1318-7

265 Леонид Люкс | К столетию «философского парохода». Мыслители «первой» русской эмиграции о русской революции и о тоталитарных соблазнах XX века | ISBN 978-3-8382-1775-8

266 Daviti Mtchedlishvili | The EU and the South Caucasus. European Neighborhood Policies between Eclecticism and Pragmatism, 1991-2021 | With a foreword by Nicholas Ross Smith | ISBN 978-3-8382-1735-2

267 Bohdan Harasymiw | Post-Euromaidan Ukraine. Domestic Power Struggles and War of National Survival in 2014–2022 | ISBN 978-3-8382-1798-7

268 Nadiia Koval, Denys Tereshchenko (Eds.) | Russian Cultural Diplomacy under Putin. Rossotrudnichestvo, the "Russkiy Mir" Foundation, and the Gorchakov Fund in 2007–2022 | ISBN 978-3-8382-1801-4

269 Izabela Kazejak | Jews in Post-War Wrocław and L'viv. Official Policies and Local Responses in Comparative Perspective, 1945-1970s | ISBN 978-3-8382-1802-1

270 Jakob Hauter | Russia's Overlooked Invasion. The Causes of the 2014 Outbreak of War in Ukraine's Donbas | With a foreword by Hiroaki Kuromiya | ISBN 978-3-8382-1803-8

271 Anton Shekhovtsov | Russian Political Warfare. Essays on Kremlin Propaganda in Europe and the Neighbourhood, 2020-2023 | With a foreword by Nathalie Loiseau | ISBN 978-3-8382-1821-2

272 Андреа Пето | Насилие и Молчание. Красная армия в Венгрии во Второй Мировой войне | ISBN 978-3-8382-1636-2

273 Winfried Schneider-Deters | Russia's War in Ukraine. Debates on Peace, Fascism, and War Crimes, 2022–2023 | With a foreword by Klaus Gestwa | ISBN 978-3-8382-1876-2

274 Rasmus Nilsson | Uncanny Allies. Russia and Belarus on the Edge, 2012-2024 | ISBN 978-3-8382-1288-3

275 Anton Grushetskyi, Volodymyr Paniotto | War and the Transformation of Ukrainian Society (2022–23). Empirical Evidence | ISBN 978-3-8382-1944-8

276 Christian Kaunert, Alex MacKenzie, Adrien Nonjon (Eds.) | In the Eye of the Storm. Origins, Ideology, and Controversies of the Azov Brigade, 2014–23 | ISBN 978-3-8382-1750-5

277 Gian Marco Moisé | The House Always Wins. The Corrupt Strategies that Shaped Kazakh Oil Politics and Business in the Nazarbayev Era | With a foreword by Alena Ledeneva | ISBN 978-3-8382-1917-2

278 Mikhail Minakov | The Post-Soviet Human | Philosophical Reflections on Social History after the End of Communism | ISBN 978-3-8382-1943-1

279 Natalia Kudriavtseva, Debra A. Friedman (Eds.) | Language and Power in Ukraine and Kazakhstan. Essays on Education, Ideology, Literature, Practice, and the Media | With a foreword by Laada Bilaniuk | ISBN 978-3-8382-1949-3

280 Georges Mink, Iwona Reichardt (Eds.) | The End of the Soviet World? Essays on Post-Communist Political and Social Change | With an afterword by Richardt Butterwick | ISBN 978-3-8382-1961-5

281 Kateryna Zarembo, Michèle Knodt, Maksym Yakovlyev (Eds.) | Teaching IR in Wartime. Experiences of University Lecturers during Russia's Full-Scale Invasion of Ukraine | ISBN 978-3-8382-1954-7

282 Oleksiy V. Kresin | The United Nations General Assembly Resolutions. Their Nature and Significance in the Context of the Russian War Against Ukraine | Edited by William E. Butler | ISBN 978-3-8382-1967-7

283 Jakob Hauter | Russlands unbemerkte Invasion. Die Ursachen des Kriegsausbruchs im ukrainischen Donbas im Jahr 2014 | Mit einem Vorwort von Hiroaki Kuromiya | ISBN 978-3-8382-2003-1

284 „Alles kann sich ändern". Letzte Worte politisch Angeklagter vor Gericht in Russland | Herausgegeben von Memorial Deutschland e.V. | ISBN 978-3-8382-1994-3

285 Nadiya Kiss, Monika Wingender (Eds.) | Contested Language Diversity in Contemporary Ukraine. National Minorities, Language Biographies, and Linguistic Landscape | ISBN 978-3-8382-1966-0

286 Richard Ottinger (Ed.) | Religious Elements in the Russian War of Aggression Against Ukraine. Propaganda, Religious Politics and Pastoral Care, 2014–2024 | ISBN 978-3-8382-1981-3

287 Yuri Radchenko | Helping in Mass Murders. Auxiliary Police, Indigenous Administration, SD, and the Shoa in the Ukrainian-Russian-Belorussian Borderlands, 1941–43 | With forewords by John-Paul Himka and Kai Struve | ISBN 978-3-8382-1878-6

288 Zsofia Maria Schmidt | Hungary's System of National Cooperation. Strategies of Framing in Pro-Governmental Media and Public Discourse, 2010–18 | With a foreword by Andreas Schmidt-Schweizer | ISBN 978-3-8382-1983-7

289 Richard Ottinger (Hrsg.) | Religiöse Elemente im russischen Angriffskrieg gegen die Ukraine. Propaganda, Religionspolitik und Seelsorge, 2014–2024 | ISBN 978-3-8382-1980-6

ibidem.eu